DK EYEWITNESS GUIDES

NORTH AMERICAN
INDIAN

Arapaho
toy horse

Tlingit
shaman's
headdress

Dakota
doll in
traditional
dress

Dakota
pipe
bag

North
Greenland
Inuit snow
goggles

Dakota
beaded
vest

Choctaw
sash

Menominee
moccasins

Eagle feathers worn in a headband by Ojibwe, a
Chippewa warrior, to symbolize his war honours –
notches were won for killing and scalping a Dakota

Unnotched feathers for scalping a Dakota killed by
another warrior – dots of rabbit fur indicate how
many bullets in his gun when he took the scalp

Winnebago
roach
headdress

Tlingit hair
ornament made
from pig's tusk

DK EYEWITNESS GUIDES

NORTH AMERICAN
INDIAN

Written by
DAVID MURDOCH

Chief Consultant
STANLEY A. FREED PhD
Curator, Department of Anthropology, AMNH

Photographed by
LYNTON GARDINER

Pair of
Omaha
calumets

DK

DORLING KINDERSLEY
London • New York • Stuttgart

In association with
THE AMERICAN MUSEUM OF NATURAL HISTORY

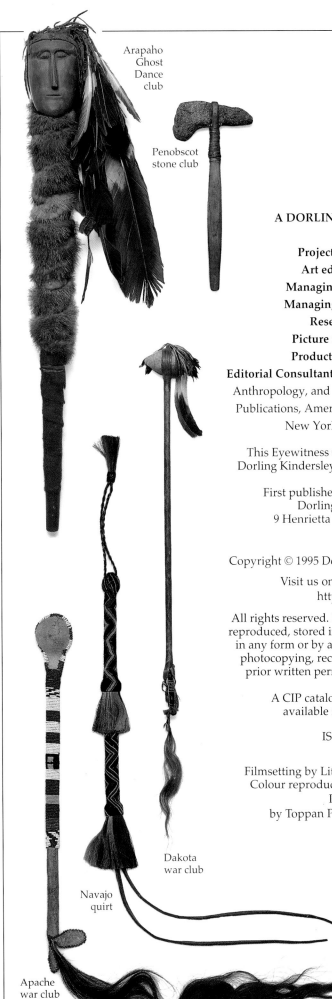

Arapaho
Ghost
Dance
club

Penobscot
stone club

Dakota
whistle

DK

A DORLING KINDERSLEY BOOK

Project editor Marion Dent
Art editor Vicky Wharton
Managing editor Simon Adams
Managing art editor Julia Harris
Research Céline Carez
Picture research Sarah Moule
Production Catherine Semark
Editorial Consultants Laila Williamson, Department of
Anthropology, and Scarlett Lovell, Director of Special
Publications, American Museum of Natural History,
New York; and Mary Ann Lynch

This Eyewitness ® Guide has been conceived by
Dorling Kindersley Limited and Editions Gallimard

First published in Great Britain in 1995 by
Dorling Kindersley Limited,
9 Henrietta Street, London WC2E 8PS

6 8 10 9 7

Visit us on the World Wide Web at
http://www.dk.com

A CIP catalogue record for this book is
available from the British Library.

ISBN 0 7513 6036 8

Filmsetting by Litho Link Ltd, Welshpool, Powys
Colour reproduction by Colourscan, Singapore
Printed in China
by Toppan Printing Co., (Shenzhen) Ltd.

Dakota
war club

Apache
tobacco pouch

Navajo
quirt

Apache
war club

Hopi bow and arrows

Contents

Blackfeet buffalo skull used in Sun Dance ceremony

Peopling of the Americas

WHO WERE THE FIRST AMERICANS? Archaeologists agree that human beings probably trekked across the Ice Age land bridge from Siberia – but they do not agree on when this happened. Once thought to be 12,000 years ago, the date might be 40,000 years ago according to some new scientific theories. Some present-day Native North Americans believe their sacred stories place their beginnings in America, just as some Christians believe human beings were created in the Garden of Eden. Archaeology shows that, however they got there, the first Americans, adapting to changing climate and environment, evolved from hunters using stone-tipped weapons to more advanced societies of farmers and artisans.

MIGRATION THEORY
During the Ice Age huge amounts of water froze in glaciers, Bering Strait became drained, and a wide low treeless plain (Beringia) connected Siberia and Alaska. About 12,000 years ago an ice-free corridor opened. Archaeologists believe that Palaeo-Indians crossed Beringia, following the corridor to open country south of the glaciers.

Beringia

Ice-free corridor

Glacier

Exposed land

Map of North America showing the first human migration from Siberia across the Ice Age land bridge

Model of an atlatl – from the Aztec word meaning "spear-thrower"

Small Clovis point

Folsom point

Larger Clovis point could measure 13 cm (5 in) in length

Bannerstone (a weight of stone) on which spear rested

ICE AGE HUNTERS
Definite proof of Ice Age human beings in America came in 1926, with the discovery at Folsom, New Mexico, of carefully shaped stone weapon points, dating from 10,000 years ago. In 1932 weapon points from an even older people, up to 12,000 years ago, were unearthed at Clovis, New Mexico.

Wooden bar up to 1 m (3 ft) long

Slate spear point from New England

A STRONGER, LONGER THROW
Hunters of mammoths, mastodons, antique bison, and giant sloths from 10,000 years ago – such as the Folsom people in New Mexico – used a special implement for spear-throwing. Now called an atlatl, it was a wooden bar in which the spear rested, a hooked end holding the butt. The greater leverage gave a much stronger, longer throw.

Copper spear point from the Great Lakes area

Grip of hide with loops for fingers

Chipped stone spear point from Tennessee

BECOMING EXTINCT
The end of the Ice Age 10,000 years ago, saw many large animals, like the mammoth, become extinct, perhaps through environmental change or over-hunting. From 5000–1000 B.C., the peoples of the Eastern forests learned to hunt woodland game. They lived in permanent settlements, were expert tool-makers (making spear points), and developed complex societies.

Copper spear point from the Great Lakes region

Polished Anasazi deer-bone spatula

Turquoise and jet inlay

DESERT DWELLERS
The Hohokam people (from the Pima word for "the vanished ones") lived in the desert near the Gila River, Arizona, c. 500 B.C. to A.D. 1500. Expert irrigators, they avoided war, grew maize, built towns, and were superb artisans, making jewellery cleverly cut from shells (left) and fine pottery (below).

WHY DID THEY DISAPPEAR?
The Anasazi (the Navajo word meaning "ancient enemy") lived on today's Arizona-New Mexico border. By A.D. 1100, they had evolved the great stone and clay buildings later to be called pueblos (pp. 46–47). Their culture faded in the late 1200s, perhaps irreparably damaged by a prolonged drought.

Pair of Hohokam shell bracelets

Red-on-buff pottery was traditional Hohokam style

Rare jet ornament found at Pueblo Bonito

Eye made from inlaid turquoise

Frog was symbol of water in Anasazi culture

ANASAZI ARTISANS
Architecture and town design were the noteworthy skills of the Anasazi, their great buildings standing today as reminders of a complex civilization. They also produced interesting pottery and were skilled in working with turquoise (above).

Mimbres pot as a burial offering was ritually "killed" by puncturing base to let the spirit escape

TRADITIONAL STYLE
The Hohokam, predecessors of the Papago and Pima (pp. 50–51), may have been an offshoot of one of the great Central American civilizations, perhaps the Maya. Their early pottery seems similar to ancient Mexican designs. About A.D. 400, they began making striking, two-colour, red-on-buff pots with simple line patterns. Later, more complex designs included animals, human figures, and their gods. The Hohokam cremated their dead, sometimes placing the ashes in these traditional vessels which were buried.

Animal head

MOGOLLON-MIMBRES
The Mogollon people (named for their mountain homeland on the Arizona-New Mexico border) lived isolated in mountain valleys, c. 300 B.C.– A.D. 1300. The Mimbres (a related group living near New Mexico's Mimbres River) produced remarkable black-on-white pottery from c. A.D. 700. Their artists later created vivid designs of every kind of creature (animal, bird, and human) and geometric patterns – often mixing them.

A vast continent

BY 1500 CANADA AND THE USA were home to about 1.3 million people. Over 11,500 years the descendants of the first Siberian migrants had diverged into more than 300 tribes. The densest population lived east of the Mississippi, in California, and the Northwest. They had evolved ways of life exploiting food resources in different environments and developed high artistic skills. Their world was constantly changing – game animals became extinct, and drought and tribal warfare led to migrations. Over the next 400 years Europeans would bring about catastrophic changes, such as loss of territory, population decline, and cultural restrictions for all Native North Americans.

THE TERROR OF THE PLAINS

In 1500 the Cheyenne were not yet feared Plains warriors (pp. 28–29). Settled in villages, they farmed and hunted in Minnesota. They migrated west only in the mid-1700s, abandoning farming and becoming nomadic horsemen dependent on the buffalo. Then an eagle-feather war bonnet (left) would be a mark of an experienced and respected warrior.

Red cloth, glass beads, and metal disc decorate headdress

Ceremonial war bonnet of Cheyenne Chief White Eagle

Fur tassel

Apache buckskin cap decorated with glass beads and metal disc

Eagle feather plumage

APACHE WARRIOR

The Apache (pp. 48–49) were newcomers in the Southwest in 1500, for they seem to have migrated from Canada about 50 years before. The Spanish explorer Francisco de Coronado (1510–1554) thought the Chiricahua group he met in 1540 were "a gentle people", but later Spaniards soon came to disagree with him!

Tlingit shaman's
headdress

*White eagle
feather*

*Magpie tail
feather*

DRIVING OUT EVIL SPIRITS

For the Northwest peoples (pp. 52–57), the spirit world affected every aspect of the tribe's life. Their shamans were revered because they could tap into the spirit world by acquiring a guardian spirit, represented by a fearsome mask with an elaborate headdress. A shaman's powers let him or her predict events, bring good fortune, and cure the sick. Because it was believed evil spirits caused illness the shaman fought fire with fire, using the guardian spirit to drive out evil.

*Swansdown surrounds
painted wooden mask,
which represents an eagle*

TWO TIMUCUA

John White – in the 1580s briefly linked with England's "Lost Colony" at Roanoke in North Carolina – used his artist's skills to portray the tribes he met in the Southeast. Later, he copied pictures of the Florida Timucua (right) made by his friend Jacques le Moyne. White was fascinated by Native peoples and helped create an image in Europe of a gentle and noble people. Sadly, by the 1700s, his still-popular pictures fed European bigotry and prejudice, so Native peoples were seen as naked, shameless, heathen savages.

Two Timucua
with traditional
body tattoos

*Roach made of dyed
animal hair – an
eagle feather was
added if a scalp
had been taken*

Map of
North America
showing the
ten different
cultural areas
of Native North
Americans

ARCTIC

SUBARCTIC

NORTHWEST

PLATEAU

GREAT
BASIN

PLAINS

NORTHEAST

CALIFORNIA

SOUTHWEST

SOUTHEAST

DRESSING FOR WAR

When village-dwelling Winnebago (pp. 22–23) left to hunt buffalo they did so on foot. If on a raid, a Winnebago warrior wore a roach headdress if he had killed but not scalped an enemy. A roach was attached by tying a braid of hair to a flat, thin plate of bone (called a roach spreader), which pressed the headdress to the head.

CULTURAL AREAS

This map shows the ten North American regions whose geography, climate, and resources distinctively shaped the cultures of the tribes who lived in them – eastern farming tribes, settled villages in the Southwest, nomadic buffalo hunters on the Plains, and Inuit in the Arctic. By A.D. 1500 Native peoples spoke over 200 different languages. In a given area two neighbours' speech might be as different as French and German – hence the wide use of sign language on the Plains.

Winnebago
roach headdress

Medicine and the spirit world

POWER FILLED THE WORLD of the Native North American. Invisible but everywhere, this supernatural force of the spirit world touched people, animals, and plants. Shamans were special men and women who could capture some of this power to manipulate the ordinary world, especially to heal the sick. Because a shaman carried healing herbs, Europeans called him a "medicine man", but for a shaman and his tribe all spirit power was "medicine". Shamans used dramatic ceremonies to help the patient's mind reject sickness. They also knew about drugs, such as the stimulant caffeine and salicylic acid (aspirin) by the Southeast's Five Tribes. Plains tribes used skunk-cabbage root for asthma and yarrow for minor wounds, both effective remedies. Shamans (like white doctors) were powerless against great European epidemics – especially smallpox, which decimated Native population from 1.3 million in 1500 to 400,000 before recovering.

Medicine pipe

Tobacco bowl would be attached here

Sinew string

Fox tail

George Catlin painting of Old Bear, a Mandan shaman

OLD BEAR
The Mandan, like other Plains tribes, believed visions brought spirit-power. To receive a vision, a Mandan would seek solitude, pray, and deny himself food until near delirium. A truly powerful vision made its recipient a shaman. Dress and equipment (above) would be dictated by the shaman's first and later visions and would, therefore, contain power.

Held by shaman during a healing ritual

Quinault carved wooden wand

HOW TO CURE A STOMACH ACHE
The Hidatsa Plains tribe dealt with indigestion or other stomach pains by hand massage or using a stomach pusher (above). With the patient laid flat, the curved end of this instrument (often made of white cedar) was rubbed against the stomach.

Animal and bird skins decorate bearskin robe

A HEALING CEREMONY
George Catlin (1796–1872) was determined to record the way of life of Native Americans before it was destroyed by whites. He made a tour of the American West (1830–36), having gained the confidence of 48 tribes, and produced over 500 vivid paintings and sketches and detailed notes. This portrait shows a Plains Blackfeet shaman performing a healing ceremony. Dressed in a bearskin robe, with the head forming a mask, the shaman danced round the patient.

Double-mouthed sea lion's head

Elk bone

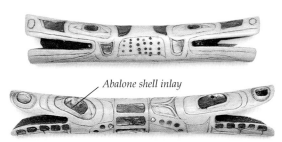

Abalone shell inlay

SHAMAN'S SPIRIT HELPER
Like all the tribes of the Northwest, the Quinault believed in a multitude of spirit beings who constantly affected the ordinary world. A shaman's powers came in part from his or her own special guardian spirit. When acting as a doctor casting out an evil spirit, a shaman would carry a carving of the guardian spirit (above).

CATCHING A SOUL
Tsimshian shamans, like those of other Northwest tribes, believed illness was caused either by an evil spirit or by the loss of the patient's soul – perhaps through a witch's spell. Therefore, one of the shaman's most important instruments was a soul catcher (right). A carved ivory or bone tube, it captured the soul and returned it to the body. Sometimes blowing through the soul catcher helped to expel the sickness.

Copper wire
wrapped tightly
round pipe stem

Wooden
pipe
stem

Clutch of
feathers
specially
dyed red

String of metal bells
which mimic sound
of thunder during
sacred ceremony

Beaded string
attaches feather
and animal hair
tassel to pipe

FIRST SIGN OF THUNDER
Most revered of the Blackfeet
sacred medicine pipes were
the thunder pipes. At the first
spring thunder, these pipes were
removed from their bundles of
sacred objects and offered
to the thunder spirit. The
ceremony asked protec-
tion from being struck
by lightning (a frequent
hazard on the Plains) and
also for the power to heal
sickness. Possessing a
thunder pipe brought
great prestige, but it was
expected that ownership
would be passed on to others.

Animal fur
decoration

Red, blue, yellow, and
green geometric
patterns were
typical Dakota
designs

Rawhide thong
for tying lid

Side seam
laced with
red yarn
over black
fabric

Dakota
medicine
box and
herbs

Eagle
feather

Roots wrapped
in paper
packet

Blackfeet
sacred thunder
medicine pipe

A REMEDY FOR EVERYTHING
In addition to resorting to
shamans with their supernatural
powers to cure illness, sick people
had available numerous common
medicines obtained from plants.
This early 1900s' Dakota medicine
box contains herbs for headache,
earache, stomach pain, bleeding,
swelling, and other ailments. The
herbs were rubbed on a tin
grater and then the powder
was steeped in hot water to
make a healing tea.

Muslin packet,
containing herbs,
tied with sinew

11

The far Northeast

Map of North America showing the Northeast: New England and the St Lawrence Lowlands, the Mid-Atlantic, Ohio River Valley, and Western Great Lakes

A LAND OF ABUNDANT CONTRASTS, the wooded Northeast stretched from the St. Lawrence River to present-day North Carolina and west to the Mississippi. Its peoples made the most of an environment rich in game and fish, while raising maize, squash, and beans, except in the very cold, far Northeast. Northern tribes, like the Penobscot and Malecite, living amid lakes and rivers, developed the birchbark canoe, much envied by their neighbours. From the early 1600s, trading furs with Europeans brought new ideas and materials. However, Northeast peoples (like the powerful Iroquois League) were drawn into the European struggle for North America in the 1700s and forced to pick sides in the American Revolution (1775–1783) and the Anglo-US War of 1812. Most saw their independence destroyed and some were completely swept away by relentless American settlement.

INGENIOUS DESIGN
Tribes like Nova Scotia's Micmac exploited the fishing resources of their lakes and rivers, using hooks, lines, bows, traps, and spears. They liked to fish at night using birch-bark torches. Attracted by the light, the fish came to the surface where they were speared from birchbark canoes.

Wooden shaft of Micmac spear lashed to three barbs by cord

Central metal barb stabs fish

KING PHILIP
In 1675, angry and fearful at the growth of European power, "King Philip" (or Metacomet), chief of the Wampanoag, attacked the New England settlements. Eventually the rising was crushed but if King Philip had formed effective alliances with other tribes, the English colonies might have been destroyed.

Wooden side barb prevents fish from struggling free

Cord ties metal blade to wooden handle, providing a handy grip when drawn toward the woodworker

A CROOKED KNIFE
Birch bark was used to make canoes, wigwams, and paper. Bark sheets were cut with knives (like this Penobscot example), holes pierced along the edges with an awl, and the sheets sewn together with spruce root to make storage or cooking vessels. Two-tone patterns were created by scraping away a dark coating on the bark's inner surface to reveal a lighter colour.

Top (right) and side (below) views of model of Malecite canoe

Low-ended canoe gives greater stability in calm waters – canoes with high bows and sterns provide protection from waves in choppy waters

Natural grain of bark running longitudinally allows sheets of bark to be sewn together more easily

Paddle up to 1.5 m (5 ft) long

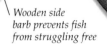

Canoe up to 7.5 m (25 ft) in length

*Decorative
shoulder
fringing*

*Beaded flowers
show European
influence*

EUROPEAN INFLUENCES
Before contact with Europeans, clothing
in the Northeast was usually made from skins,
sometimes decorated with painted symbols or
dyed porcupine quills. European settlers brought
new materials and decorations, such as woven
cloth, glass beads, and tailored coats and trousers.
The peoples of the Northeast adopted many of
these innovations. Northeastern men traditionally
wore a skin coat with painted decorations.
This Penobscot buckskin jacket shows
European influences – a tailored shape
and elaborate glass-bead embroidery.

*Stone club
slotted into
wooden
handle*

DEER SLAYER
Though the forest
peoples were skilled
at hunting, it was an
uncertain business. Aid
was sought from the spirit
world through sacred
charms and by rituals to
contact the spirits of the
slain animals. The chief
hunting weapon was the
bow. However, an arrow
might not be fatal, so a
stone club (like this Penobscot example) was used for
killing a wounded deer.

*Struts made
from split
logs of white
cedar*

DECORATED DEERSKIN
Like all the peoples of the northeastern forests, the Penobscot wore
moccasins made from deerskin, which
were usually decorated. The influence
of the Europeans shows in the use of the
many coloured glass bead decorations
and the adoption of flower designs.
Floral motifs were copied from white
settlers and became widespread in the
clothing of the Northeast. Both men and
women wore the same style of moccasin.

A DESIGN TRIUMPH
The best canoes were made from bark of
the white birch, growing only in Canada and the
most northeastern USA. The framework was made
from white cedar, split with hammers and wedges,
then covered with large sheets of bark laced together
with roots and waterproofed with resin from the black
spruce. Light enough to be carried, it could take a load
of 1,800 kg (4,000 lb). It was instantly adopted by
European explorers and fur traders from the 1600s.

The League of the Iroquois

OUT OF THE NORTHERN WOODS, early in the 1600s, there emerged the strongest political and military force in North America. Five tribes – the Mohawk, Onondaga, Seneca, Oneida, and Cayuga – ended their destructive feuding and formed the Iroquois League. Each tribe remained self governing, but collective decisions were made by a representative Great Council. Though the members were men, they were chosen by the elder women of the tribes, who also had the power to remove them. The League was conceived to bring peace, but it became a formidable war machine because it was able to mobilize its forces effectively, dominating much of the Northeast. Even as late as the mid-1700s, it could still hold the balance of power in the colonial wars between the French and the British.

CORNPLANTER
Son of a Dutch trader-father and a Seneca mother, Cornplanter (?1740–1836) fought Americans during the Revolution (1775–1783). Later, this respected Seneca chief became a tireless spokesman for peace, negotiating many treaties.

Stone celt (blade) later replaced by steel

TRIBES AT WAR
For the Iroquois, war was usually a matter of short raids, with weapons like bows and war clubs. But involvement with Europeans, competing for the fur trade, changed this. In 1649 the Iroquois League, as allies of the Dutch, virtually destroyed the Erie and Huron tribes, who supported the French.

Rattle made from a whole turtle shell

MOHAWK MUSIC
Music for the Mohawk, as for other eastern peoples, mostly depended on drums and rattles. A turtle-shell rattle was made by drying out the animal, then cleaning out the shell – being careful to leave the head, tail, and legs intact. After this, pebbles were inserted and a wooden handle added.

HIAWATHA – A HERO
In the late 1500s, the prophet Dekana-widah, despairing at constant inter-tribal warfare, saw Iroquois union in a vision. The Mohawk Hiawatha then travelled ceaselessly between the tribes, persuading them to unite. *Hiawatha*, Henry Longfellow's (1807–1882) famous poem, gives no indication of the charisma and diplo-matic skills of this remarkable leader.

Belts woven from wampum could be many metres long

Purple beads were twice as costly as white ones

Elm-bark covering

Iroquois warclub made in typical "rabbit's hind-leg" style

THE COLOUR PURPLE
Strings of purple and white tubular shell beads, called wampum, were used as symbolic gifts at marriages, to console the bereaved, or as an invitation to ceremonies such as peace negotiations or a war alliance. White was the colour of peace, black for gloomy matters, but purple was the most valuable. Realizing the high value placed on it by the tribes, Europeans manu-factured wampum from shell, using it in trade as money. Then they began to counterfeit it in glass. As money, it became debased and fell out of use.

Model of a four-fire, eight-family longhouse

MAGNIFICENT MASKS, MYSTERIOUS MEDICINE

The False Face Society was a group of healers who used the powers they derived from the spirit world to cure ailments mostly involving the head, shoulders, and limbs (such as headache). Ceremonies, held at the patient's invitation in the longhouse, were short because of the great power of the False Faces. A cured patient was obligated to become a member of the Society, to help others. Every spring and autumn the False Faces would visit each Iroquois household to purify it spiritually and exorcise disease.

Metal eye piece

Each mask was carved into a trunk of a living basswood tree – when nearly finished, the sculpture was cut away, the face hollowed out, and features painted

Features of mask varied widely, depending on face seen in dream – mouth could be smiling (above) or crooked (left)

Cayuga
False Face

Seneca
False Face

Cobs of maize drying on storage racks in roof rafters

All families in a longhouse related through the women

Long strands of horsehair, used as ornate decoration of each False Face

LONGHOUSE STYLE
The Iroquois lived in longhouses, up to 7.5 m (25 ft) wide and 45 m (150 ft) long, built with a frame of wooden poles covered by elm bark. Compartments with low sleeping platforms for up to 12 families lined the sides. Shared cooking fires were spaced up the central aisle. Granary pits for maize were dug into the ground at key points within the village.

The three sisters

MAIZE (CORN) WAS LIFE for tribes throughout the eastern woodlands. Producing starch to make energy, it could provide 75 per cent of the human body's food needs. Many maize varieties were grown (the Iroquois raised fifteen), but none required much labour. No further care was necessary after planting the seed, except for scaring off birds, until the harvest. In the same field, beans were often planted, twining up maize stalks, and squash, which choked weeds and kept the ground moist. The Iroquois believed these crops had spirit beings and called them "the three sisters". Dried and stored, maize, beans, and squash guaranteed food supplies so more time could be devoted to hunting, trading, war, and ceremonies.

AUTUMN TREAT
Ripening in the autumn, pumpkin squash was a valuable vegetable. English colonists learnt its use from Native Americans and invented sweet pumpkin pie, traditional at Thanksgiving.

Iroquois wooden bowl containing dried beans

BOWL OF BEANS
Depending on environment and accidents of history, many different varieties of bean were grown across the continent. However, all had the same important qualities. They were a good extra food source because they had high amounts of proteins and vitamins (particularly Vitamin B, essential for the body to convert starch to energy). Equally important, they could be dried and stored for long periods (even years) without spoiling.

Ojibwa bark basket with dried rings of Sauk and Fox squash plaited together

Seneca wooden pestle

Mohawk mortar made from hollowed-out tree trunk

DRIED SQUASH
Squashes (similar to courgettes and marrows) grew thoughout the summer, when they were eaten fresh, providing an important source of Vitamin C, essential for general health. They could be cut into strips or rings and sundried, or hung up whole inside the dwelling until dry, then stored with beans and maize.

Iroquois harvesting basket containing cobs of Oneida dried maize

GRINDING MAIZE
Iroquois women shelled the kernels from the maize cob with deer jawbones, then boiled the kernels in lye (made from boiled ashes) to soften the skins. The lye and skins were next washed away in a special basket and the kernels dried. These were turned into meal by laborious pounding with a mortar and pestle (left).

"CORN" ON THE COB
Some maize had to be saved for the lean winter months. Cobs were dried and hung in the longhouse – some were shelled and the kernels dried and stored in bins or underground granaries. Dried maize could be made into porridge, or lightly roasted, then ground and eaten with maple sugar, honey, or fat.

MID-WINTER CEREMONIAL

The most solemn of the Iroquois ceremonies was held at mid-Winter, around the first of February. Messengers would stir the ashes of each longhouse fire, symbolizing the start of a new year. At the end of the four-day ceremony, the secret societies performed ritual dances. Among these was the Husk Face Society, whose members believed they were linked to spirit beings particularly connected with farming. Wearing sacred masks made from braided and sewn maize husks, they danced to persuade the spirit world to ensure a good harvest and the birth of many children.

Holes left for eyes and mouth

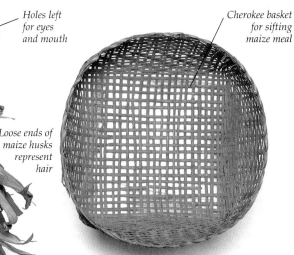

Cherokee basket for sifting maize meal

Loose ends of maize husks represent hair

FINE TUNING

The contribution of Cherokee men to crop raising was clearing the land. Trees were felled by cutting a circle in the bark (the dead trunk was later burned). Women then hoed the soil and made small mounds in which to plant the maize. Usually, two crops were sown – one for summer eating and a second for autumn, to be dried and stored for winter. After husking and washing, the maize was ground into meal. This was then shaken through a sifter basket, like a modern sieve, to remove the coarse fragments.

Iroquois Husk Face made of individual maize husk braids sewn together to form a face

Round stone pounder

Square stone mortar

Iroquois wooden bowl

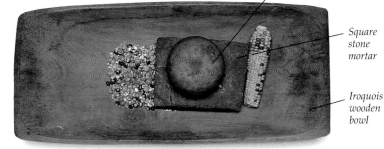

MAKING A MEAL OF IT

After husking, drying, and shelling, Iroquois women had a long, hard job in making maize into meal. In addition to the wooden mortar and pestle (far left), dried kernels of corn could be cracked and ground between two stones, a wooden bowl serving to catch the meal.

SPRING PLANTING

In 1564, French explorer Le Moyne made drawings of the Timucua in Florida. His picture of them planting spring maize looks more like French peasants than Native Americans. The Timucua used hoes with fish-bone heads (not iron-headed mattocks) and the women planted seeds in holes, not loosely scattering them.

The Mid-Atlantic Seaboard

A LAND OF WOODED PLAINS and lush valleys extended along the Mid-Atlantic Seaboard. Its people raised maize, hunted in the forests, and lived in villages of bark-covered, domed (or arch-roofed) dwellings. They were led by sachems (chiefs) who ruled by consensus. In 1585 John White, briefly part of the English colony at Roanoke (North Carolina) before it mysteriously disappeared, made paintings of the Secotan. These were later published as engravings, which produced the Europeans' stereotype of "Indians" for the next 200 years. When the English settled the colony of Virginia, they met with the strong Powhatan alliance, which nearly destroyed them. More powerful than the Powhatan were the Delaware, a confederation whose influence in the 1600s stretched far to the north and west, though their power was later broken by the Iroquois.

Delaware effigy of a woman, simply carved in wood

Elaborate decorations (silver crosses and buckles) show strong European influence

A SECOTAN VILLAGE
John White (pp. 8–9) painted this scene of a typical Secotan village in 1585. Shown are houses of bent saplings covered with bark and woven mats, surrounded by a defensive palisade (a circle of upright posts). The houses with sleeping platforms resemble those of the Iroquois to the north. The building with the cupola is a temple. Eventually, the Secotan disappeared from their territory in North Carolina and were succeeded by other tribes.

A DOLL FOR HEALTH
The Delaware believed in the universal presence of the Great Spirit and also in a world filled with lesser spirit beings, which shaped their lives, fortunes, and health. Prayers, offerings, and ceremonies were meant to seek the help of these beings. This wooden image is a woman spirit-guardian of health. Every autumn, the Delaware honoured her with a feast, presents, and the sacrifice of a deer.

WOODLAND ART
With abundant wood at hand, Eastern tribes naturally used it for many household utensils, such as bowls, spoons, and ladles. Woodworking was a task for men. To make hollow vessels like this bowl, the wood was first charred, then the burnt part scraped away with a stone (later iron) knife. Carved from the burled (knotty) parts of elm and maple, these objects were both useful and an expression of woodland art.

Simply carved wooden Delaware serving bowl and spoon

Paddle intricately carved with a star

Handy hook topped with a crown

More ornately carved with turtle, horse, and horseshoe

Delaware wooden food stirrer

Bottom filled with stones to sink basket to river bed

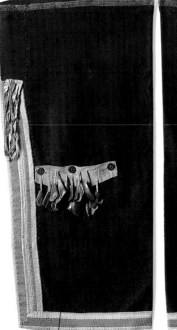

Delaware leggings made of woven cloth

WEARING APPAREL
Most clothing was made from animal skins, particularly deerhide. Men, taught from boyhood to ignore rain and chilly weather, wore only a breechclout (a flap worn front and back and held up by a belt) and moccasins in the warmer months, together with buckskin leggings. Women wore a waist-to-knee skirt over knee-high leggings. In winter both men and women added a fur robe. European contact brought woven cloth (left), which was sometimes substituted for skins, and new clothing patterns, such as jackets and trousers.

POCAHONTAS'S WEDDING
In 1607 Captain John Smith (1580–1631), from the English colony of Virginia, was captured by the chief of the Powhatan. Smith's life was dramatically saved by the pleadings of the chief's daughter, Pocahontas (1595–1617). Kidnapped by the English, she met and later married John Rolfe (1585–1622). This marriage kept the peace between the English and the Powhatans until the chief's death in 1618.

Decorated with deerhoof rattles and silk-ribbon appliqué

TRAPPING FISH
Fish were an important addition to forest game all over the Eastern woodlands, not least because they could be caught all year round. Fish were speared, shot with bows, or taken with hook and line. Where some species migrated upriver to spawn, they could be caught by using nets, weirs, or traps (below).

Loosely woven splint construction

Fish swam into opening, but could not turn round once inside

Large handle for ease of carrying awkward shape

Powhatan fish trap

TRADITIONAL DRESS
Crowded from their 17th-century homeland in Pennsylvania and New Jersey by colonial settlement, by 1830 most Delaware had finally settled in Indian Territory (Oklahoma). Traditional dress persisted among women, as this photograph of a mother and daughter from the early 1900s shows. Nellie Longhat (far right) and her mother are wearing cotton dresses with a cape decorated with silver brooches, bead-embroidered moccasins, and an accumulation of bead necklaces.

The Ohio River Valley

THE FERTILE LANDS OF THE GREAT VALLEY drained by the Ohio River and its many tributaries offered a rich environment for two great pre-historic cultures – the Adena and later the Hopewell which together spanned about 1500 years to A.D. 500. The Hopewell culture spread from the Eastern Great Lakes to the Gulf of Mexico and west of the Mississippi. They created large earthworks – almost all we know about the Hopewells comes from excavating these burial mounds. Spectacular artists and artisans, they imported exotic raw materials from a vast trade network. The Hopewells faded as quickly as they had arisen and simpler hunter-farmer tribes slowly took their place. In the 1700s, France and Britain, with their tribal allies, fought for control of the Ohio Valley as the key to dominating North America. From the 1790s, relentless white American settlement created a short-lived, inter-tribal resistance movement led by the Shawnee statesman, Tecumseh.

Shawnee cloth storage bag decorated with stitching and appliqué

Mother nursing a baby

Distinctive top-knot hairstyle is typically Hopewell

GRAVE IMAGES
The Hopewell people buried their dead surrounded by their wealth – ornaments, jewellery, fine stone tools, and pottery. Some of these may have been made specially as grave items, which might include small clay figurines (above). These give us our only knowledge of the Hopewell people's appearance, clothing, and ornaments, though probably only of those rich enough to afford large burial mounds.

Wrap-around skirt was usual costume for Hope-well women, a style that continued well into the 1800s

IN THE BAG
The Shawnee were a powerful force in the Ohio Valley in the late 1700s and tried to become a barrier to American westward expansion. However, they were defeated by General "Mad Anthony" Wayne in 1794 and, in 1831, they sold what was left of their lands and moved to Oklahoma.

Unusual style in which bird effigy faces away from smoker

Tobacco loaded into bowl in bird's back

STRIKING BIRD
Hopewell stone-carving showed the same artistry as their other work. Most striking were stone pipes, carved in the shape of animals or birds, such as this raven (above). Most, called platform pipes, had a base on which the carved figure containing the bowl for tobacco rested. The smoker drew the smoke through a hole bored through the base.

Massive stone pipe found in western Tennessee

Smoke drawn through hole behind bird's body

Decorated with 291 nickel-silver brooches

Silk ribbon appliquéd to cloth wraparound Miami skirt

Extensive beadwork

Coloured yarn balls

Decorated Huron sheath made of moose hide

HURON HUNTERS
The Huron were long-standing enemies of the Iroquois who dealt them a stunning defeat in 1649. James Fenimore Cooper (1789–1851), who wrote *The Last of the Mohicans*, made the Iroquois the villains of some of his stories. This Huron skinning-knife sheath is decorated with beads, appliqué stitching, and animal hair.

Fine beadwork

MIAMI ALLIANCES
Allied with other tribes, the Miami suffered the common defeats of the 1790s and in the War of 1812. However, trade with whites continued and brought items such as wool, silk ribbon, metal brooches, and glass beads. Miami women thought that using these gave prestige to their clothing and developed techniques to get striking effects, such as the skilful appliqué and nickel-silver decoration on this woollen skirt from the early 1800s.

A POTAWATOMI POUCH
For Native Americans, the great issue of the late 1700s was to maintain the Ohio River as the boundary between white settlers and them. Like the Miami and Shawnee, the Potawatomi fought to stop the settlers. After several defeats, they and other tribes signed peace treaties in 1815. Despite hostilities, they traded with whites for new clothing materials, so that only bags, tobacco pouches (above), and moccasins continued regularly to be made from deerskin.

THE GREAT TECUMSEH
Tecumseh (1768–1813) used his great political skills to forge a tribal alliance opposing white advance into the Midwest. With his shaman twin brother Tenskwatawa (1768–1836), he argued that land could be ceded only with the consent of all the tribes. Despite his belief in peaceful negotiation, in 1811 white forces destroyed the league at the Battle of Tippecanoe (Indiana). Embittered, Tecumseh joined the British (who made him a general) in the War of 1812 against the USA, in which he was killed.

Western Great Lakes

The peoples of the western great lakes (an area west of Michigan) took full advantage of their access to both woodlands and prairies. In the summer, the women of tribes such as the Sauk and Fox planted maize and squash while the men hunted buffalo. The Menominee harvested huge quantities of wild rice – their name comes from the Chippewa name for this plant. In winter, the tribes were semi-nomadic hunters, using portable lodges of poles and reed mats as they followed game. The tribes traded with each other but also were regularly at war. From the early 1600s, a powerful force was the Midewiwin, a shamans' secret society devoted to healing and encouraging correct behaviour as a guarantee of good health.

Male doll given husband's name, and female doll the wife's name

Love medicine is placed in breast of each Menominee doll

Each grizzly bear claw separated by three blue beads

MEDICINE DOLLS
Shamans used human figures as "medicine" to control others' behaviour. The Menominee used "love dolls" (above) to ensure a husband and wife were faithful to each other and tied the dolls face to face. The Potawatomi, however, used dolls as charms, to make one person fall in love with another.

SWEET AS MAPLE SUGAR
Maple sugar was greatly valued, used not only on fruit and grains but also on meat and fish as a seasoning. Collection began in late March, when each tree was gashed and a cedarwood spout inserted to allow the sap to drain into a birchbark bucket. Whole Menominee families moved into the woods, where each had its own group of trees and a special wigwam.

Ojibwa sap skimmer

Ojibwa wooden trough and Menominee ladle (far left)

MAKING MAPLE SUGAR
First the sap was boiled. Before iron pots were available, boiling was done by dropping heated rocks into birchbark containers. After boiling and skimming, the resulting syrup was strained through fibre matting and poured into a wooden trough. As it cooled, it was worked to and fro with a ladle until it formed granules.

SUGAR CONES
Much of the sugar was stored in birchbark containers for use during the year. Some might be forced into moulds, such as these Ojibwa cones (right), much like Europeans once made a conical sugar loaf from cane sugar.

BEAR CLAW NECKLACE
Necklaces of grizzly bear claws were greatly prized, not least because of the difficulty of persuading their original fearsome owners to part with the main components! Usually the property of a chief or renowned warrior, they were often passed from one generation to another.

CHIEF KEOKUK
Unlike his rival Black Hawk (1767–1838) who fought a hopeless war against settlers in 1832, Sauk chief Keokuk (?1780–1848) realized that his people had to leave Illinois. His tribe honoured him for establishing their claim, and that of the politically affiliated Fox, to territory in present-day Iowa. His realism is shown in his avoiding the fate of Black Hawk's followers, destroyed in their war with the US government.

THE SUPERNATURAL
Individuals who could gain extraordinary power from the spirit world became shamans. Through a vision, a spirit being taught the shaman the use of many "medicines" (bones, roots, skins), which were stored in a medicine bag (above). Shamans used their power to cure illness and bring success in war and hunting.

Collar made from otter skin

Eagle feather decoration

Bear claw necklace of the Fox tribe

Metal bowl held tobacco

WAR OR PEACE PIPE?
Tobacco was thought to have special powers, so it was used in offerings to please spirit beings. The Menominee also believed smoking increased their wisdom. At important ceremonies, tribes smoked the sacred calumet, which was passed around clockwise. Because this often marked the end of fighting, the calumet is usually called a peace pipe, but it was also used in the war council.

Sacred Menominee calumet

The settled Southeast

RICH IN FLORA AND FAUNA, with fertile lands, and a mild climate, the Southeast was an ideal environment. As skilled builders, artisans, and farmers, with a wide knowledge of medicine, the Southeastern peoples created a flourishing civilization. From A.D. 800–1500, the Southeast's Temple Mound Builders developed large towns, traded widely, and held great ceremonies. The rulers lived luxuriously while commoners toiled. The human-made, flat-topped mounds in the region are the community sites of this vanished people. The historic Natchez tribe, which also built mounds topped by temples, may have survived the Mound Builders. Contacted by the Europeans in the late 1600s, the Natchez, under pressure from colonists to cede land, fought back. Three wars with the French in the 1700s destroyed their nation, scattering the survivors throughout the Southeast.

Map of North America showing the Southeast region

THE ANNUAL BUSK

The Green Corn Ceremony (Busk) was the most important rite of the Southeast. Held when the maize ripened, it offered thanks for the harvest and marked the beginning of a new year. It involved ritual purification, dancing around a sacred fire, and a celebratory feast.

Yuchi feather fan carried by dancers

Thatched roof

Pole frame

Sleeping platform

Mud wall

Model of a Natchez house

Colour of fan echoed colour of Busk – dancers and spectators alike were dressed in white

SUNS AND STINKARDS

Successor to the Temple Mound Builders, the Natchez amazed French explorers with their complex hierarchical society and elaborate ceremonies. Ruled by an all-powerful monarch, the Great Sun, Natchez society was divided into Suns, nobles, honoured men, and commoners (stinkards). The main village had a temple on a mound that sheltered an eternal flame and houses such as the one above.

Wooden lacrosse stick measured up to 1 m (3 ft) long

A TWO-HANDLED, THREE-LEGGED POT

Women made the pottery in the Southeast. The clay was cleaned and mixed, then long clay cylinders were layered on top of a small clay disc. A wetted shell was used to smooth the clay, thin the walls, and shape the pot. Before firing, the pot was polished with a smooth pebble and designs cut in with a pointed wooden tool.

Finely etched decoration

Catawba pot based on ancient techniques

SHELL GORGET
The Temple Mound people often used decoratively incised shells as ornaments. This gorget (a plate hung around the neck to rest on the chest) has the image of a long-nosed god. Unfortunately, because these people had no writing, our knowledge of their beliefs is fragmentary.

Hole for string to allow gorget to be hung from neck

Skin-covered Yuchi lacrosse ball stitched together with sinew

Loosely woven webbing made of thin strips of hide

Perfectly rounded chunkey disc made of highly polished stone

Heavily woven webbing showing more intricate style

A CHUNKEY STONE
A popular Temple Mound Builders' sport was "chunkey". One player rolled a polished stone disc down a court 30 m (100 ft) long. Then he and his opponent threw wooden lances to mark where they guessed the disc would fall over. The game was still played in the Southeast when the Europeans arrived.

Each stick made from a single piece of bent wood

HOW TO PLAY LACROSSE
Though known to many Native North American peoples, the stick-and-ball game that French explorers called lacrosse was played with fanatical enthusiasm in the Southeast. Teams had 100 players each, often many more. Each player used two sticks with webbed ends to catch and throw the ball, made from wood or stuffed deerskin, ultimately aiming to hurl it between the opponents' goalposts.

Thin strips of hide lash the two ends together

Each player allowed to hold two lacrosse sticks

Special designs painted on face and body

Mane worn around neck

Beaded belt

Yuchi lacrosse stick

DRAMATIC PAINTINGS
American artist George Catlin (1796–1872) painted several dramatic pictures of lacrosse in 1834. This portrait shows Thirsts-for-Stone, an outstanding Choctaw lacrosse player, wearing his best game outfit (right). He would have drunk sacred medicine and performed ritual dances before the game. The women of the village, accompanied by medicine men, sought aid from the spirit world for their team through dances and singing.

Long, rigid horsetail

George Catlin painting of a Choctaw ball game

LITTLE BROTHER OF WAR
Lacrosse, as played in the Southeast, was so violent that the Indians called it the "little brother of war". Serious injuries were commonplace and players sometimes were killed. Challenge matches between villages or tribes attracted perhaps 1,000 rival supporters. Spectators betted heavily on the result.

The "Five Civilized Tribes"

A REMARKABLE CIVILIZATION had grown up in the lush Southeast by the late 1500s. The tribes lived in planned villages, were skilled farmers as well as hunters, and had advanced medical knowledge. Three hundred years later they had adopted American agricultural methods, put their laws in written form, and many had become Christians. All this made no difference to the whites who were determined to seize their tribal lands. In the 1830s, the Choctaw, followed by Cherokee, Creek, Chickasaw, and finally Seminole (called the "Five Civilized Tribes" by the whites), were forcibly moved to Oklahoma, many dying on the trail.

Fine beadwork fit for a chief

DRESSING UP
Seminole dolls show how women, up to the early 1900s, combed their hair around a frame, and wore skirts and capes of strips of cotton cloth in contrasting colours. A girl was given a string of beads when young and added to them throughout her life, until they almost reached her ears – and weighed several pounds.

THE EAGLE DANCE
Before contact with Europeans, a most important Cherokee ceremony was the Eagle Dance, held as part of the rites celebrating both peace and war. Dancers wore eagle feathers on their heads and waved eagle feather wands to music from drums and rattles.

Smaller feathers attached with sinew to either end of wooden handle

CHIEF OF THE CHOCTAW
The Choctaws' original home was in Mississippi and Louisiana until most were removed by the US government to a reservation in Indian Territory, which was later called Oklahoma (the Choctaw name for "red people"). This sash was worn at his wedding in 1871 by a chief of those Choctaw who managed to stay in Louisiana.

Feathers decorate Cherokee Eagle Dance wand

Small entrance leading into windowless house

A LITTLE HUT BY THE WATER
In hot, humid Florida, such as the Everglade swamps, the Seminole lived in open-sided dwellings (chickees). Made from palmetto poles with thatched roofs, these huts were built on platforms to avoid flooding from the heavy rains.

Wall made of dried mud smoothed onto gate-like framework of small poles

26

MAKING MUSIC
Both ceremonies and games were accompanied by music made by drums and rattles. A water drum had a deerskin stretched over a hollow log, containing water so that it resonated. Rattles were made from dried turtle shells, cattle horns, or gourds.

Creek rattle made from hollowed-out gourd filled with maize kernels or small stones to make sounds

Conical roof made up of several poles running from the circumference at the bottom of the structure

THE UNDEFEATED SEMINOLE
Originally mostly Creek from Georgia and Alabama, the Seminole (left) fled to Florida (their name means "runaway") in the 1700s, where they were joined by many runaway slaves. The Seminole fought two wars with the US. The second (1835–42) began with the government's efforts to remove them to Oklahoma. Led by the great Osceola (below), the Seminole fought US forces to a standstill. Although many Seminole surrendered in 1841–42 and were sent west, others remained in Florida's Everglade swamps undefeated. A treaty was signed with them only in 1934, ending possibly the longest war in history.

George Catlin painting of Osceola

A MEETING HOUSE
Creek village dwellings were carefully organized into open summer houses and warm winter lodges. The council of elders met in a square surrounded by sun shelters in summer and in a round house, up to 7.5 m (25 ft) high, in bad weather. This council house was also used for ceremonies and festivities.

SEMINOLE HERO
In 1835, enraged by an agreement to move the Seminole to Oklahoma, Osceola (1804–38) killed a rival chief to become leader of those who were determined to stay in their Florida homeland. Small bands of guerilla forces were led by Osceola against 10,000 US troops until he was captured through dishonourable US trickery.

Roof made from thin tree trunks, covered with bark sheeting to provide extra protection from heavy rains

Model of Creek council house in which elders are holding a meeting

Central fire

The Great Plains

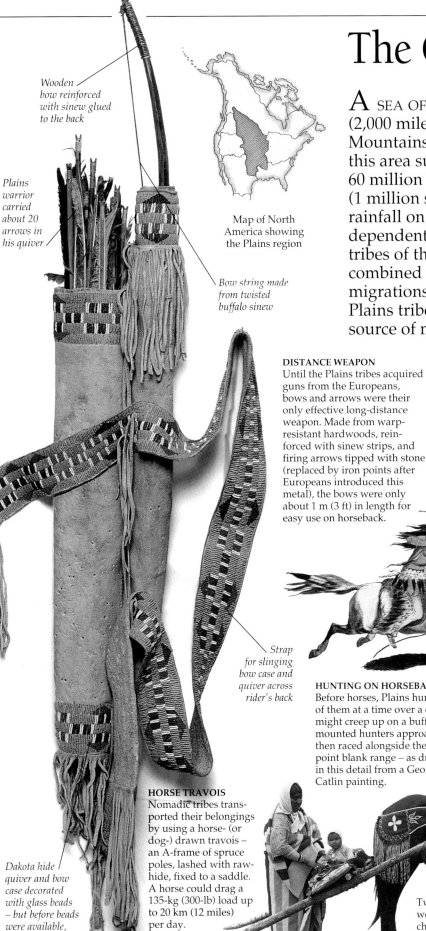

A SEA OF GRASS stretches more than 3,200 km (2,000 miles) north to south, between the Rocky Mountains and the Mississippi River. In 1800 this area supported about 150,000 people and 60 million buffalo, all sharing 2.5 million sq km (1 million sq miles) of territory. With sparse rainfall on the western Plains, tribes there were dependent on the huge herds of buffalo, unlike tribes of the better-watered eastern Prairie who combined farming with buffalo hunting. Buffalo migrations dictated the pattern of life for the 30 Plains tribes. The buffalo meant not just a crucial source of meat, but their hides, hair, and horns made dwellings, clothing, tools, and utensils. Before the Spanish brought horses to the Southwest in the 1500s, nomadic Plains tribes travelled and hunted on foot. Of all Native North Americans, Plains peoples were the finest horsemen. Their riding skills dominated the style of their incessant warfare.

Wooden bow reinforced with sinew glued to the back

Plains warrior carried about 20 arrows in his quiver

Map of North America showing the Plains region

Bow string made from twisted buffalo sinew

DISTANCE WEAPON
Until the Plains tribes acquired guns from the Europeans, bows and arrows were their only effective long-distance weapon. Made from warp-resistant hardwoods, reinforced with sinew strips, and firing arrows tipped with stone (replaced by iron points after Europeans introduced this metal), the bows were only about 1 m (3 ft) in length for easy use on horseback.

Strap for slinging bow case and quiver across rider's back

HUNTING ON HORSEBACK
Before horses, Plains hunters killed buffalo by stampeding hundreds of them at a time over a cliff. A lone hunter disguised as a wolf might creep up on a buffalo until within bowshot range. Later, mounted hunters approached stealthily until the herd ran, then raced alongside the fleeing animals to fire at point blank range – as dramatically shown in this detail from a George Catlin painting.

Long travois poles were also used to make a tipi

HORSE TRAVOIS
Nomadic tribes transported their belongings by using a horse- (or dog-) drawn travois – an A-frame of spruce poles, lashed with rawhide, fixed to a saddle. A horse could drag a 135-kg (300-lb) load up to 20 km (12 miles) per day.

Dakota hide quiver and bow case decorated with glass beads – but before beads were available, flattened, dyed porcupine quills were used

Two Blackfeet women and child with horse travois

PLAINS BALL GAME

The Plains peoples played games which tested qualities important to their way of life – such as speed and strength. The most popular game among women was shinny. Two teams, armed with curved or straight sticks, struggled to get the ball (below) past each other's goalposts. The ball could be batted or kicked but not touched with the hand. Men also played, and sometimes a men's team might challenge a women's.

Arapaho decorated hide ball used in game of shinny

HAVE TIPI WILL TRAVEL

For the nomadic hunting tribes, the tipi was a highly practical dwelling, cool in summer and warm in winter. Constructed from a cone of long poles covered with buffalo hides sewn together, it could be erected by two women in an hour. About 5 m (15 ft) in diameter, it comfortably housed a family, their bedding, and belongings. Tipis were usually decorated with traditional painted designs.

Design painted on tipi could come from mythical dream creatures such as an otter

Two sticks used in a Plains Cree throwing game

Up to 20 straight poles bound together at top formed cone shape

Each pole up to 7.5 m (25 ft) long

Smoke flap adjusts either to keep in heat or to air out tipi

Arrow with eagle's feather denotes lightning

Entire crow belt represents the Thunderbird spirit being

Feathers represent birds of prey fighting over dead bodies in war

Buffalo hide (from 8 to 20 skins) draped over pole skeleton

Bells represent sound of thunder

Wooden lodge pins removed when tipi folded up for travelling

Model of Arapaho Grass Dancer

GRASS DANCE

In the late 1800s a new ceremony (the Grass Dance) spread throughout the Plains tribes. Originally an Omaha ritual which recalled men's courage and achievements in war, it became a social dance with songs and costumes. To a people threatened with the destruction of their way of life, the Grass Dance became and remains a symbol of Native North American solidarity.

Tipi set up with entrance facing east, because of prevailing westerly winds

The Dakota (Sioux)

THE LORDS OF THE NORTHERN PLAINS by the mid-1800s were the Dakota. Called Sioux by Europeans (from the Chippewa word for "enemy"), they had been forced westward in the 1700s from their Western Great Lakes homeland by well-armed Chippewa. The Dakota were made up of seven independent groups, ranging from Minnesota west to the Upper Missouri River. The largest of the Plains tribes and outstanding warriors, the Dakota terrorized their Indian enemies and offered fierce resistance to whites. Their lives depended on the buffalo – and the end of the great herds meant the end of their independence. However, between 1862 and 1877, they forcefully resisted US advance into their lands and inflicted the most famous defeat on the US army by Native Americans near eastern Montana's Little Bighorn River.

USING A BOW AND ARROW
Dakota children were taught proper behaviour and encouraged to imitate adults. They were treated with much affection and rarely punished. They were expected, however, to learn skills at a young age. Boys practised shooting with half-sized bows and arrows (above), first at targets, then at small game, and began hunting seriously in their early teens. Girls were expected to help their mothers in brutally hard outside work.

Geometric beadwork style was favoured by the Dakota

BETTER THAN BAREBACK
Though Plains tribes long rode bareback, a saddle and stirrups gave better stability and control. The Dakota "pad saddle" had hardly any cantle to support the rider's back, or pommel at the front. It was made from two pieces of tanned hide, stitched together and stuffed with buffalo or deer hair. Stirrups, usually wooden, were attached by a rawhide strap.

Heavy, cotton flank strap (cinch)

Unadorned fringed central flap

Dakota hide saddle

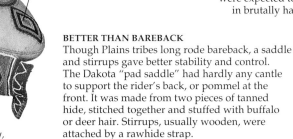

Hide strap for tying items to saddle

Buffalo raw-hide covers wooden stirrup

Detail from 1881 pictograph of the Battle of the Little Bighorn, painted on a buffalo hide (below)

THE BATTLE OF THE LITTLE BIGHORN
Gold seekers invading the sacred Black Hills in South Dakota, guaranteed to the Dakota by treaty, brought about war in 1876. A US Army unit moved against a huge force of Dakota and Cheyenne, not realizing their numbers. General George A. Custer (1839–76) impetuously attacked with an advance guard. On 25 June, 1876, he and his 215 men were all killed.

DEATH ON THE PLAINS
The Dakota did not bury their dead. Instead, the body was wrapped in a buffalo robe and placed beyond the reach of wild animals on a platform supported by poles. Warriors had their weapons and medicine pouch hung beside them, women their important household utensils. Relatives mourned beside the body.

Unusual warfare design

Lance with beadwork, buffalo fur, horsehair, and feathers

Eagle feather headdress

Horsehair tassel

Porcupine quills were dyed and flattened, before sewn with sinew onto hide bag

THE ART OF QUILLWORK
Before white traders arrived with beads, Plains women took great pride in their quilling skills. Women's saddlebags were made in pairs to hang on each side of a saddle, or to store household articles in a tipi.

OLD MAN OF THE PLAINS
Ceremonial dress for a Dakota elder in the mid-1800s marked his status. His headdress of eagle tail feathers (thought to have spirit power) could be worn only by a proven warrior. His costume was completed by beaded leggings and quilled moccasins. A headdress such as this was presented to Sitting Bull when he became a chief of the Teton Dakota.

Elaborately beaded cradleboard with metal stud, horse-shoe, and bell decoration

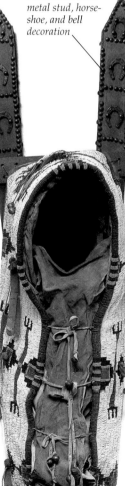

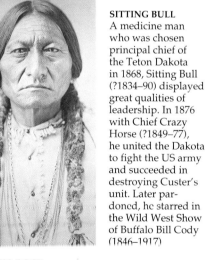

Poncho-style shirt, made of mountain sheep-skin, has scalp-locks, quillwork, and is painted blue and yellow

SITTING BULL
A medicine man who was chosen principal chief of the Teton Dakota in 1868, Sitting Bull (?1834–90) displayed great qualities of leadership. In 1876 with Chief Crazy Horse (?1849–77), he united the Dakota to fight the US army and succeeded in destroying Custer's unit. Later pardoned, he starred in the Wild West Show of Buffalo Bill Cody (1846–1917)

CRADLE WILL ROCK
A Dakota baby spent much of its time in a cradle-board. A lace-up skin bag on a wooden framework, it could be strapped to a mother's back, hung from a saddle, tied to a travois, or just propped upright. A decorated cradleboard like this would usually be made by the sister of the baby's father.

Mandan and Hidatsa

Model of a bullboat – a circular, skin-covered vessel

FERTILE RIVER VALLEYS and open prairies, hot summers and numbingly cold winters – the Mandan and Hidatsa learned to exploit and adapt to their homeland on the upper Missouri River in North Dakota. They built permanent earthlodge villages on the high banks above the river and farmed the bottom lands. Half of their food came from crops such as maize, the rest from the vital summer buffalo hunt. To deal with winter cold, they built separate lodges along the river, where there was plenty of wood for fuel. As hunter-farmers the Mandan and Hidatsa were typical of the prairie tribes, just as the Dakota were typical of the high plains tribes. They were fierce warriors, which was necessary to protect themselves from marauding bands of Dakota.

ACROSS THE RIVER
Settled on the Plains rivers, the Mandan used bullboats. Made from a (bull) buffalo hide stretched over a willow framework, a bullboat was light but strong enough to carry heavy loads. Able to move in very shallow water, it was usually a one-person craft. The paddler knelt and dipped the paddle straight in front. To prevent the boat from spinning, the buffalo's tail was left on – attached to a piece of wood, it acted as a stabilizer.

BRAIDED EARS
Raising crops was women's work, but men sometimes helped clear land or harvest the crops. A Plains woman, helped by her female kin, could farm 1.2 ha (3 acres) each year and grew maize, beans, squash, sunflowers, and melon. Planting was done in spring, and harvesting in September when the ears of maize were husked (outer leaves of cobs removed) – the best were braided into strings, which were hung up to dry, then stored in pits in the earthlodge's floor.

INSIDE A MANDAN LODGE
In 1833–34 a German prince, Maximilian von Wied-Neuwied, toured the American West to study the tribes. To make a visual record of his findings, the prince took Swiss painter Karl Bodmer (1809–93) on the trip. They travelled far up the Missouri River and met the Mandan and Hidatsa tribes. Bodmer's painting (left) of the interior of a Mandan lodge shows warriors, with dogs, horses, and weapons to hand, viewed by the dim light of the chimney hole.

Chimney hole, covered by bullboat framework, lets in light

CLOSE TO THE EARTH
Earthlodges were dome-shaped, up to 15 m (50 ft) wide. Built mainly by women, they were home to their extended families together with horses, dogs, and belongings. An earthlodge was thought to be sacred, so its construction was accompanied by many ceremonies. All social activities and housekeeping took place round a central fireplace.

Entrance was a covered walkway with an inner skin door

Roof of wooden rafters topped with willows, grass, and sod

Carved knife in horned eagle feather headdress represents a battle with a Cheyenne chief

Karl Bodmer's portrait of Four Bears – the last great Mandan chief

CHIEF FOUR BEARS

Prince Maximilian believed the Mandan were descendants of the Welsh prince Madoc, who supposedly sailed to America in 1170 – a tale long proved to be false! During the winter of 1833–34, so cold that his paints froze, Karl Bodmer produced several fine pictures, including this portrait of the Mandan chief, Mato-Tope (Four Bears). Mato-Tope must have become used to posing for his portrait, since the artist George Catlin (1796–1872) had painted him the previous year.

Antler horns tied to wooden handle by animal sinew

Wooden, hide-covered handle

Hidatsa hammer made by covering a round stone with buffalo hide

INVALUABLE KNOWLEDGE

The story of the Hidatsa has been strikingly told by Buffalo Bird Woman (1839–?1920s) and her son, Edward Goodbird (1869–1938), who were photographed with Son of a Star (right) in 1906. Much of their story was related to an anthropologist (someone who studies cultures) working in collaboration with the American Museum of Natural History. Besides invaluable knowledge of tribal life and customs, their account detailed the move to a government reservation (1885–88) and the problems this brought.

Canopy, made from half a tipi cover, provided privacy in the sleeping area

Sacred shrine was located opposite the entrance at the rear of the lodge

MAKING PEMMICAN

Pemmican was the all-purpose emergency food of the Plains with a very long shelf-life! It was made by mixing together dried buffalo meat, boiled fat, and chokecherries (bitter berries from local shrubs). For pounding the meat until near powder and cracking the bones to boil out the fat, a large stone hammer was used. Pemmican was very nutritious and would keep for years.

A SIGN OF THE TINES

For weeding the fields of maize, the Hidatsa preferred rakes with deer antler tines (prongs of a fork). This was partly because they believed wooden rakes produced the maize worms which damaged the crop. Tribal stories also told of deer weeding the garden of their ancestor, Eternal Grandmother, and of how she made the first rakes from their cast-off antlers.

War and peace

ON THE GREAT PLAINS, warfare was part of life but it rarely involved great battles between tribes. Instead, small bands of warriors made raids to steal horses or to avenge a death, but always to win honour. Audacity and courage were greatly respected and deeds were graded on a system of "coups" (the French word for blows), which included taking a scalp, stealing a horse, or touching an enemy in battle. War was a bloody and deadly business, which inflicted serious casualties on each tribe. Tribal warfare was a test of personal courage and spiritual power, rather than a battle for territory and political control conducted by disciplined soldiers. Native North American war customs left them at a great disadvantage when fighting white and black regiments.

THE MASSACRE AT WOUNDED KNEE
In the turmoil created by the Ghost Dance (below left), on 23 December, 1890, 470 US 7th Cavalry troopers were guarding 340 surrendered Sioux. A tense situation exploded and both sides opened fire. Over 64 soldiers and 200 Sioux (including unarmed women and children) were killed – the Sioux bodies were dumped in a mass grave. Wounded Knee became a symbol to Native Americans of their mistreatment by whites.

Metal blade fitted around wooden handle

Carved face is symbol of owner's supernatural helper who appeared in Ghost Dance vision

WAR PARTY
A Plains raiding party was armed with bows and arrows, shields, lances, clubs, and scalping knives. A war club might have a blade, spike, or shaped stone for the head. Tomahawk-pipes, like this Dakota example, were used more as prestigious ceremonial objects than as weapons.

Wand made from wooden tube or hollow reed

Arapaho Ghost Dance wand

Headdress was a circle of magpie and turkey feathers

Wand with white shaft and mottled feathers represents the female calumet

VISION OF HOPE
By the late 1800s, the Plains peoples, in despair on reservations, turned to a new ceremony, the Ghost Dance. Born in a Paiute prophet's (Wovoka, pp. 40–41) vision, it promised the end of the whites and a return of the buffalo. Ghost Dancers sought visions in which they visited the spirit world and met dead relatives. In later dances, they carried objects seen in the vision (left).

DOG SOCIETIES
Various Plains tribes, such as the Blackfeet, Hidatsa, and Gros Ventre, had military Dog Societies. On a tour of the West in 1833–34, Swiss artist Karl Bodmer (1809–93) painted this striking portrait of the Hidatsa Dog Dancer, Pehriska-Ruhpa (Two Ravens). Hidatsa Dogs were "contraries" and did everything backwards – for example, if a warrior was meant to attack in battle, he was told to flee.

Eagle feather
decoration

Special protective
symbol painted
on Blackfeet
shield

Quanah Parker,
Comanche chief,
and his wife
Tonasa, c. 1892

COMANCHE CHIEF
Such were the reputation and political
skills of Quanah Parker (?1845–1911),
war leader of the feared Comanche,
that he became their first overall
chief after peace in 1875.
An outstanding politician, he
worked for the tribe's interests
with the US government, getting
better treatment for the
Comanche on their Oklahoma
reservation. He was also made a
judge in the new Federal Court of
Indian Offences in Washington.

Hide shield made from
buffalo's neck, hard-
ened by steam and
smoke, then painted

Wand with blue shaft
and white feathers
represents the
male calumet

Tassel
made of red-
dyed horsehair

ON THE DEFENSIVE
Worn on the left arm, leaving hands free for weapons,
a Plains warrior's shield was tough enough to stop an
arrow or deflect a lance. A ritual of songs and prayers
was involved in its construction, invoking protection
by supernatural powers.

On underside of
each Omaha calumet
(sacred pipe) is a
straight, red groove
representing the
path of happiness

Feathers of an
eagle (a bird
with tireless
strength)
symbolize war,
when a calumet
is waved by a
dancer during
a war ceremony

WAR OR PEACE?
Among the most sacred
objects of Plains peoples were
calumets. A ritual could involve
an older man adopting a younger
one as his son. Calumets presented
to another tribe guaranteed peace,
because war could not be waged
against relatives. The recipient of a
calumet was promised long life,
good fortune, and prosperity.

Red flannel
symbolizes
Sun's rays

White string for
Moon's rays

35

The Sun Dance

Buffalo skull specially painted and placed at the altar of the Blackfeet Sun Dance

AT THE TIME of the summer buffalo hunt, when each tribe had reunited after scattering widely in the winter, most Plains peoples held the Sun Dance – the greatest of their ceremonies. The rites differed among tribes, such as the Dakota, Crow, and Blackfeet, but the purpose was to thank the Great Spirit for past help and pray for future blessings. The ceremony fulfilled a promise by one person (a pledger) to show gratitude for aid from the spirit world, although it was for the benefit of the whole tribe. The ritual lasted several days and nights. Tribes built a sacred Sun Dance Lodge, where a sacred cottonwood tree, forked at the top, was at the centre of the ceremony. Found by a warrior, it had been cut down by specially virtuous women. After days of ritual dances, finally came several kinds of ordeal. Volunteers chose to accept self-imposed pain to have a personal vision. It was also hoped that the Great Spirit would spare the whole tribe from future suffering.

Slow Bull, a Plains medicine man

THE GREAT SPIRIT
The Plains peoples' world was filled with spirits who possessed power and inhabited places, persons, animals, even objects. Some tribes believed all power came from the Great Spirit. Individuals might sing to the spirits to plead for their aid, or by privation seek a vision which would transmit to them some sacred power. Those who gained great power became "medicine men", tribal leaders, and advisers.

MOST POWERFUL MEDICINE
The Crow Sun Dance was held for someone seeking vengeance for the killing of a relative. A ceremonial doll was suspended by a hoop from the sacred cottonwood. Crow sacred stories tell of a warrior grieving for his family who was killed by enemies. A vision showed him how to make the doll, which would ensure revenge.

Feather headdress decorated with fur and beads

Feather headdress adorning Dakota effigy

SACRED EFFIGIES
The Dakota attached special objects to the fork of the sacred cottonwood in the Sun Dance Lodge as the focus for a ritual dance. These objects, made of raw-hide, were symbolic and included effigies, or simple cut-out figures, of a man (symbolizing the enemy) and a buffalo. The ritual ended with dancers firing arrows at the figures.

Crow deerskin doll is stuffed with sweetgrass

Simple buffalo effigy cut from a piece of rawhide

RESPECT FOR BUFFALO
As the vital resource at the centre of their way of life, most Plains peoples had the buffalo feature prominently in their versions of the Sun Dance. Both Blackfeet and Dakota painted buffalo skulls and decorated them with sage and grass.

Cylindrical case for storing the Blackfeet Natoas bundle, which included a sacred headdress

Digging stick

Eye and nose cavities were stuffed with sage and grass, as a symbolic offering to the buffalo to wish them successful grazing

Rawhide fringing

Detail from a painting by Frederic Remington (1861–1909)

AN AGONIZING ORDEAL
In the Sun Dance ordeal, all dancers fasted and endured privations. But some chose to have rawhide thongs driven on wooden skewers through their chest muscles and attached to the fork of the sacred cottonwood pole. Swaying to the music and blowing eagle bone whistles, or even suspended from the fork, they gained release only when the skewers tore out of their flesh. Disturbed by this practice, the US government banned the whole Sun Dance from 1904 to 1935.

A SACRED WOMAN
In addition to cutting down the sacred cottonwood tree, women sang during the various dances, brought the dancers presents, and took part in the ordeals. But most important, the Blackfeet ceremony depended on a Sacred Woman for the rituals. Whoever had pledged the Sun Dance had to buy a Natoas bundle, which was transferred to the Sacred Woman in a special rite. Kept in a rawhide case, the Natoas bundle contained several sacred objects such as face paints and rattles, but the most important were a headdress and a digging stick.

The high Plateau

THE GREAT PLATEAU (stretching from the Cascade Mountains in the west to the Rockies in the east and south from the Fraser River to mid-Oregon, western Wyoming, and Idaho) was home to 25 tribes. Most lived in tipi-like lodges in summer and in winter, earth-covered, part-underground houses. Their main food was salmon and edible roots. Some became traders and bartered skins, hemp, and horn bows for buffalo skins, superior robes, and decorated objects from the Plains. The Plateau peoples used horses only from the 1700s, but soon became famous for breeding and trading them. Trade brought prosperity which ended only with pressure from white expansion after the 1830s.

Thompson deer target made of rushes

Map of North America showing the Plateau region

CEREMONIAL DEER
The death of a member of the Thompson (named after an explorer of the 1800s) tribe was marked by a special ceremony. A rush figure of a deer, suspended from the house roof, was shot at for four days with a special bow made from mountain maple with a bark string and unfeathered rosewood arrows. The target, bow, and arrows were never used again.

Feathers decorate bow made from mountain sheep horn

Bow made of mountain maple wood

Bark string

Ceremonial arrow, made of rosewood, was never feathered

Parfleche filled with wedding gifts given by groom's family to bride's was a Nez Perce custom

Longest arrow was 1.4 m (57 in) long

Thompson ceremonial set of bow and arrows, used when a tribal member died

Sinew string

Wooden practice arrow is untipped

Rawhide thong fastener tied two end pieces (the lid) together

Thompson boy's practice bow and arrow set

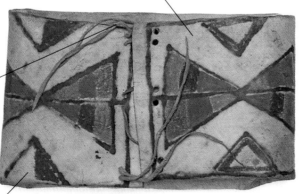

Typical geometric designs painted on Nez Perce hide parfleche

AN INGENIOUS CARRY-ALL
A parfleche was an ingenious folding container widely used throughout the Plateau and Plains. It was hung from a saddle and large enough to carry food (generally buffalo meat) and clothing. A strip of rawhide was folded and creased to make a base and two sides, then folded again one-third from each end. These end pieces were bent over to form a lid. Like other work with skins and hides, making parfleches was a task for women. Though the Nez Perce made their own, the Plateau tribes particularly valued parfleches from the Plains.

PRACTICE MAKES PERFECT
The best Plateau bows were made from the horn of mountain sheep. Stronger and more resilient than wood, sheep horn provided greater thrust when string was pulled – thus arrows had greater range and more accuracy. Boys were expected to develop their hunting skills very young, first shooting at stationary targets, then hunting small game such as rabbits. Plateau horn bows became important trade items, greatly valued by the Plains tribes who thought them much superior to their own.

Red and black geometric design appliquéd to Thompson hide saddle bag

THE GREAT CHASE

Clashes with whites escalated into the Nez Perce War of 1877. The band of Chief Joseph (c. 1840–1904) fought a series of running battles with increasingly larger forces of the US Cavalry and local volunteers. The Nez Perce consistently outfought their enemies in a chase lasting four months and covering over 2,600 km (1,600 miles), until they were forced to surrender only 48 km (30 miles) short of sanctuary in Canada.

Chief Joseph

A REVOLUTION

The horse revolutionized the Plateau peoples' way of life. It extended the range of their summer migrations and spread their trade down into California and deep into the Plains. As a result, they brought back not only bartered goods, but many of their neighbours' customs. However, they did not adopt the Plains travois for transport. Instead they used pack saddles and saddle bags, such as this double one from the Thompson tribe who lived in southern British Columbia.

Antler spike

RAIDING PARTY

The Thompson tribe used to raid their neighbours for booty, revenge, and honour, much like most Native North American peoples. This two-handed war club is crudely decorated, showing a lake with three warriors nearby. The notches at each end were probably ornamental, but may have been for tallying numbers of enemy killed, just as Western gunfighters were alleged to notch their guns.

Thompson birch wood war club also used for hunting beaver

Hide fringing

Notch perhaps denoted how many enemy or beaver had been killed with this club

IN THE BAG

The Nez Perce were famous for their maize husk bags. Made from twisted hemp fibre, twined without using a loom, the bags were decorated with cords made from the inner parts of maize husks. Cords were dyed with colours made from natural materials to produce typical geometric designs, with a different design appearing on the reverse side of the bag. Flexible, flat containers, maize husk bags were used to carry foodstuffs, roots, and berries. After horses, they were the Nez Perce's most important trade goods.

The Great Basin

A BAKING DESERT IN SUMMER, lashed by storms and snow in winter, the Great Basin's resources were always meagre. Nine tribes – scattered over 1 million sq km (400,000 sq miles) – had adapted so well to their environment that their way of life endured for some 10,000 years. Without agriculture and living on wild foods ranging from insects and seeds to lizards and deer, the ingenuity of these migratory people is easy to miss. They needed no permanent homes as they migrated with seasons, gathering in large encampments during pinenut harvests and rabbit drives. After gold was discovered in 1859, their lives changed drastically.

Map of North America showing the Great Basin – Nevada, Utah, Idaho, Oregon, Wyoming, and Colorado

FAMOUS BASKET WEAVER
The Great Basin tribes were expert basket weavers, particularly the Washoe, whose products were greatly valued by white buyers. Datsolali (?1835–1925) was the most famous of all Native American basket weavers. Her baskets showed control of difficult shapes and displayed traditional patterns involving extra-fine stitching.

Nevada Washoe basket maker Datsolali (white name Louisa Keyser)

PAIUTE PROPHET
In 1888 a Nevada Paiute shaman, Wovoka (white name Jack Wilson, ?1856–1932), began to prophesy that by using a new ceremony (the Ghost Dance which spread rapidly to the Plains) the white man would be swept away, the buffalo return, and the old ways restored. Though his message stressed non-violence, the white authorities reacted with brutality.

UTE BEADWORK
The Utes' homeland was on the edge of the Plains, so they adopted the neotraditional Plains ceremonial costume. This combined a European-style garment with imported glass beads decorated in traditional designs (right). White pressure soon destroyed their hunting and raiding way of life – by the 1870s most Utes had been forced on to reservations.

Cloth strip edging garment shows white influence in style, although basic material is deerskin

Coloured beads forming geometric design show fine craftwork of this Ute child's coat

Northern Paiute duck decoy made from bundles of tule reed

Plant fibre ties

Deerhide fringing

DUCK DECOY
The Northern Paiute of northwestern Nevada hunted any game available, including rabbits and marmots. In the spring, migrating birds (such as ducks) were hunted with the help of duck-shaped decoys made from tule rush bundles tied together with plant fibre. Floating realistically on reed marshes, within range of the hidden hunters' bows, they convinced the ducks it was safe to land.

HOLDING A BABY
A cradleboard left the mother's hands free for most tasks. If some accident caused a board to fall or tip over, the projecting top protected the baby's head.

Hoop, made of hide, slipped over mother's head

Useful strap for carrying cradleboard

ENDURING COURAGE
Paiute interests were vigorously defended by Sarah Winnemucca (1844–91). With some white schooling, she became official translator between the Paiute and unsympathetic, government-appointed Indian agents. Later she campaigned for white support in the East. Her 1883 autobiography is an indictment of white brutality, as well as a tribute to her people's enduring courage.

Bottom of Paiute cradleboard made from twigs and a wooden crossbar over a wooden base

Glass beads decorate soft hide covering

Long hide fringing to drain off rain

Umbilical cord hidden inside Ute lizard-shaped pendant

GOOD LUCK CHARM
Sometimes personal ornaments had a purpose. The umbilical cord of a newborn child was often put in a beaded bag, which was hung on the cradleboard or worn like a locket to ward off bad luck. The bags were shaped like a lizard or turtle because these creatures represented a long life.

Woven fibre of yucca plant

BABY CARRIER
Like the Plains tribes, the Paiute used cradleboards to carry their babies. The frame was made of thick twigs and a covering of soft animal skin. Laced into it, the baby was in a secure but comfortable carrier which could ride on the mother's back or be tied to a saddle. Even if just propped upright, it meant that the baby was always able to see its surroundings.

SUMMER SANDALS
In summer, most Basin peoples went barefoot, but some tribes made sandals from coarsely woven tree bark. Sometimes the Southern Paiute made buckskin moccasins, or sandals woven from yucca fibre. These were made according to a traditional design of the Kaibab band of the Southern Paiute.

Californian hunter-gatherers

NATIVE AMERICANS found California as attractive in the 1760s as their American successors did in the 1960s. The reasons were simple. Except for the southeastern desert, the climate and resources made life easy. Warfare was rare and farming almost unknown, the people preferring to be hunter-gatherers. Isolated by deserts and mountains from the war-like tribes to the east, the 50 tribes lived on fish and game, but seeds (especially acorns) played a major role in their diet. Their ceremonies petitioned the spirit world to ensure food and health. The arrival in 1769 of the Spanish establishing missions in the south began the erosion of this way of life, but the American Gold Rush of 1849 in the north destroyed it.

THE MODOC WAR
In 1864, Kintpuash (Captain Jack) led a group of Modoc who refused to accept their new reservation, resulting in the Modoc War of 1872. The US Army besieged Kintpuash and 80 men for six months near Tule Lake. After violating a peace parley, Kintpuash surrendered and was hanged.

FEATHER BUNCH
The Maidu, nicknamed "Digger Indians" by the Europeans (because they searched for edible roots to supplement their acorn diet), lived in part-underground dwellings, up to 12 m (40 ft) across. At some of their ceremonies, both men and women wore feather bunches (right).

Maidu dance plume, or bunch (worn on crown of head), made of quills, feathers, wood, and string

Single piece of curved wood forms basic frame of Pomo flail

Elaborate design on ceramic doll echoes tattoos painted on a Mohave warrior

Closely woven netting made from willow

DESERT PEOPLE
The Mohave, typical of the Yuman tribes along the lower Colorado River, farmed the bottom land, relying on the annual flooding of the river for raising crops. By the late 1800s, confined to a reservation, they were selling souvenirs, like these ceramic dolls (above), at a nearby railroad station.

GATHERING SEEDS
The Pomo lived between the ocean and the Coast Range. Their dwellings, each home to several families, were 9-m (30-ft) long pole frameworks covered with thatch. Though expert hunters and fishermen, the most important part of their diet was acorns, ground into meal. They also ate seeds, roots, and berries. Women used flails (right) to knock seeds into a collecting (burden) basket.

Each crane
feather
attached to
crown by
twine

Circle of half
feathers form
the crown

*Simple bead
decoration*

*Unusual feather
decoration on
Pomo basket-hat*

BASKETRY HAT WITH FEATHERWORK
The Pomo have become widely regarded as
outstanding basket makers. Unlike most Native
North American peoples, Pomo men as well as
women wove baskets. Employing four or more
materials, some for working in coloured patterns,
the weavers used both the coiling technique and
four different kinds of twining. Particularly
unusual was the idea of decorating the baskets by
attaching brightly coloured feathers to the surface.

CEREMONIAL FEATHER CROWN
The Maidu of California's Central Valley wore elaborate feather
decorations for their ceremonial dances. In a dance called lo'li,
only the women took part. They sometimes wore feather
bunches (far left), but always an elaborate feather crown called
a unu'ni. Men alone participated in the dance that followed
and they also wore the unu'ni crown (above).

*Longer
the shell,
greater
the
value*

THE LAST OF THE YAHI
In 1911 the last survivor of the isolated Yahi
tribe, long believed to have died out, appeared
in a northern California town. He was "adopted"
by anthropologists at the University of
California, who named him Ishi (Yahi for
"man"), in order to learn about his way of
life. Ishi died of tuberculosis in 1916.

SPENDING MONEY
Far to the north, on Vancouver Island, strings of dentalium shells
(above) were highly valued ornaments. Brought south by traders
of the Tolowa tribe, they were used as a form of money by many
of the California peoples. But the Pomo preferred to make a rival
currency from the white mineral, magnesite, or from clamshells.
Most northern tribes made purses from elk antlers (top),
which were strikingly decorated.

The stunning Southwest

THE SOUTHWEST IS A LAND of great majesty and spectacular contrasts, of mountains and desert, scorching heat in summer and cold in winter. Its peoples can trace their ancestry back to forbears who lived here over 2,000 years ago. Some of their stone and clay villages have been continuously occupied for over 1,000 years. In this arid land, the Pueblo peoples learned to irrigate their crops from the little water available. Their rituals were closely connected with persuading the beings of the spirit world to bring rain. So too were those of the Papago of the desert to the south. Though not warlike, the Pueblos had to defend themselves against Navajo and Apache.

Map of North America showing the Southwest region

Painted wood Zuni lightning symbol set up in a kiva altar

Bird-animal design on coiled basketry Havasupai bowl

Typical geometric decoration

PRAYING FOR RAIN
Both Zuni and Hopi Pueblo peoples lived bounded by rituals that connected them to the spirit world. Every August the Hopi held a nine-day Snake Ceremonial to bring the rain that ensured a good harvest. Snake sticks (symbols of lightning that comes with the rain) were set up in a kiva altar. At the ritual's end, painted dancers held live snakes in their mouths, then released them into the desert.

PEACEFUL LIFE IN AN ISOLATED CANYON
For nearly 900 years, the Havasupai have farmed Cataract Canyon in Arizona, using skills learned from the Hopi and water for irrigation from the Colorado River. Isolated in the canyon, they have no tradition of warfare.

PAPAGO POT
Like their cousins the Pima, the Papago were descended from the Hohokam people who lived over 2,000 years ago in settled villages in what is now Arizona's border with Mexico. In tribal life, men were responsible for raising the usual crops of squash, maize, and beans, while women wove baskets and made pots.

Unusual effigy of a tattooed woman shapes this Papago pottery vessel

Native desert frog was inspiration for bowl's decoration

Traditional black geometric design on a light background

ANCIENT ART
A tradition of pottery making among Pueblo peoples stretched back to their ancient ancestors in the region. Styles in design vary among the Pueblos, but are always highly decorated in traditional colours of red, black, and white, with either geometric or representational designs.

Four step-shaped corners, each modelled in shape of frog, decorate this large, elaborate Zuni bowl, which once belonged to a rain priest

Sinew ties lash cover to Taos Pueblo shield – both made from dyed animal hide

Decoration depicts mounted warrior carrying similar looking war shield

Typical Pinto horse descended from wild mustangs

Simple, tipi-shaped decoration

Feathers could be attached to a war shield in strips (as here) or in a circle (as on decoration)

Eagle feathers traditionally decorated war shields, but wild turkey feathers were also used

AMERICA'S FIRST APARTMENT HOUSE
The ancient Anasazi abandoned their pit dwellings, c. A.D. 750, to build pueblos. In New Mexico's Chaco Canyon lie the ruins of one of the greatest – Pueblo Bonito. Once a giant semi-circular building of 700 apartments, rising in terraces, it housed 1,200 people and overlooked a plaza containing two underground ceremonial chambers (kivas).

PUEBLO REVOLT
In 1528, nearly a century before other Europeans attempted to settle on the continent's eastern shore, Spanish invaders looking for gold penetrated the Southwest. Missionaries, soldiers, and brutality followed. In 1680, Popé (a Taos Pueblo medicine man) united all the Pueblos in a revolt, driving out the Spanish for 12 years. Though defeated, the Pueblos have preserved their religion and many traditions to this day.

The Pueblo peoples

PASSING THE TEST
Hopi girls were fit for marriage on passing tests of women's skills. Then they were allowed to style their hair in complicated squash blossom coils.

ON THE WINDSWEPT TABLETOP ROCKS towering above the desert and along the Southwest's few rivers, stand stone and adobe settlements. Today Native Americans inhabit some 30 villages from the Rio Grande to northern Arizona. The first Spanish explorers called the inhabitants Pueblo (village) people, but they were not a single tribe. The villages were independent and the people (like Hopi and Zuni) spoke different languages. From early times they have raised crops of beans, squash, and maize. Kachinas (spirit beings entering the bodies of selected villagers who wear masks and perform sacred dances) guide their lives. They are embodied only in men, who also govern the community. Women own all property which is inherited by their daughters.

AMAZING BIRD
From c. A.D. 500, the Anasazi people of the Southwest created small pottery figures of birds and animals. Remarkably similar figures were produced by Zuni potters 1300 years later (above).

CEREMONIAL BOWS AND ARROWS
On 26 June (five days after the summer solstice) begins the elaborate Hopi ceremony called Niman. It is held to ensure a successful harvest. For 16 days, solemn rituals mark the return of the kachinas to the spirit world, with prayers for rain. The departing kachinas offer the villagers symbolic gifts, including ears of maize and bows and arrows (far left).

Natural pigment decorates wooden rabbit stick

BOOMERANG THAT ISN'T
In the autumn and winter, rabbit hunting is both a sport and a ritual ceremony for the Hopi community. A mile-round circle of hunters contracts until rabbits can be hit with throwing sticks (left). These are flat, curved pieces of wood, often decorated, which act like a non-returning boomerang.

Narrow strips of sinew glued to back of wooden bow for extra strength

Wooden kachina doll represents Aholi who accompanies Chief Hopi Kachina, Aototo

Feathers typically decorate heads of kachina dolls

Feather from a bird of prey

Maria Martinez' matt-black-on-polished-black pots have become famous this century

FAMOUS POTTERY
For 900 years Pueblo peoples have developed a highly individual style of decorated pottery. San Ildefonso Pueblo traditionally produced geometric designs in two colours. Here in 1919 Julian Martinez invented a matt-black-on-polished-black design for pots made by his wife Maria.

Horns and other animal forms sometimes appeared on masks of kachina dolls, like those of kachina dancers

Kachina doll given as gift from kachina dancer who pretends to threaten the child and demands food – but if appeased the child is unharmed

NOT A TOY
Kachina dolls were not toys but a vital part of the education of every Pueblo child. These dolls, specially carved to represent the different types of kachina, taught children about the appearance and roles of the many kachinas. Kachina doll carving was most highly developed by the Hopi and Zuni.

Nakachok – a painted wooden Hopi kachina doll

Nataska, a Hopi kachina doll, helps discipline erring children

Apache and Navajo

THE ARID MOUNTAINS and deserts of the Southwest became home to the Apache and Navajo, who may have migrated south from the far northwest in the 1400s. Hunters and warriors, they first raided their Pueblo neighbours and later the colonizing Spanish, pushing north from Mexico. From both they learned important agricultural skills. The Navajo combined sheep raising, farming, and raiding, until local American forces under Kit Carson (1809–68) forced their surrender in 1864. Rebuilding their way of life, they added silver-working to their arts. Some Apache, learning from the Pueblo villagers, took up farming, but most remained hunter-raiders. Feared by other tribes and Europeans as the fiercest warriors in the Southwest, they faced their final defeat in the mid-1880s.

BRAVE WARRIOR
Geronimo (1829–1909) was his Mexican name, but his Apache name (Goyanthlay) meant "the Yawner". He became the most famous Apache warrior and fought the American invasion of Apache lands in the 1860s. He was eventually caught in 1877 and confined on the San Carlos reservation in Arizona. On his escape in 1881, he resumed raiding – to the terror of both Mexican and American settlers. He was photographed (above, far right) just before he finally surrendered in 1886.

BEST FOOT FORWARD
As an alternative to wearing moccasins with separate hide leggings to protect their legs from thornbrush, Apaches wore a one-piece soft boot, or "long moccasin", made from antelope or deer skin. Usually, men's long moccasins reached to just below the knee, while those of women extended above it.

Clothing made of hide

Glass bead denotes European influence

Head on Apache war club made of stone

Delicately coloured beadwork decoration

Hide tie for fastening child's long moccasin below the knee

Fine beadwork decoration

Metal stud decoration

Wooden shaft covered in rawhide for a firm grip

Navajo whip made from dyed horsehair

FAVOURITE DOLL
Toys of Apache children, like those of children everywhere, imitated the adults' world into which they would grow. This rag doll has its hair arranged in the Hopi style worn by an unmarried girl. When an Apache girl entered puberty, a four-day ceremony was held, with ritual singing alternating with feasting. Like the Hopi, an Apache girl was taught her future responsibilities by an older woman and ran a ritual race to prove her strength and courage. After this, she was ready for marriage.

INTO BATTLE!
Like all Native Americans, the Navajo and Apache knew nothing of horses until they met Spanish colonists in the 1500s. However, they quickly learned to use and breed them – particularly for warfare. The Navajo whip (far right) is very similar to the quirt (from the Spanish *cuerta*) used by American cowboys and Mexican *vaqueros*. The Apache war club was a good close-quarter weapon – this example (near right) is particularly handsomely decorated.

Upper bar

Shed rod

Coloured woollen yarn

Wooden batten separates upright threads

Comb beats cross threads into place

Motifs evolved from the 1870s, including diamond shapes

A TRADITIONAL WEAVE
Navajo beliefs tell how Spider Woman (one of the Holy People and a spirit being) first taught women how to weave. Skills are passed down from mother to daughter in a tradition which has lasted for generations. Tools, like the batten to separate the warp (up-thread) and the comb, to beat in place the weft (cross-thread), were often handed on. All property in Navajo clans passed from mother to daughter.

Tassel decoration made from hide

Wool anchors woven rug to lower bar

BEAUTIFULLY WOVEN
The Navajo first learned weaving skills in the late 1600s from the Pueblo peoples, using wool from sheep originally raided from the Spanish. By the mid-1800s, Navajo textiles were traded all over the western USA. Blankets were woven in intricate patterns and traditional colours, which changed over time. From the late 1800s, American merchants encouraged the weaving of rugs with pictorial designs, like the one above. This form of Navajo art is now well known and valued worldwide.

Beaded Apache tobacco pouch fringed with metal decoration

Cow's tail attachment, specially dyed red

FINE BEADWORK
The Apache did not become known for pottery like the Hopi, nor weaving and silverwork like the Navajo. Apache women, however, produced beautiful baskets, made from willow rods, and fine beadwork, as shown in this elaborate tobacco pouch.

Papago and Pima

IN THE PARCHED DESERTS of what is now Arizona and northern Mexico, over 2,000 years ago the Hohokam people built irrigation systems to raise crops. Their descendants are the Pima and Papago (their name for themselves, O'Odham, means "the People"). Using this inherited knowledge of river irrigation, the Pima settled in villages by the Salt and Gila rivers, raising maize, squash, and beans, adding wheat around 1700. Their surplus food became so great, they supplied California miners and the Union Army during the American Civil War (1861–1865). The desert-dwelling Papago had to rely on seasonal flood water for farming and so stayed semi-nomadic. From the fermented fruit of the saguaro cactus they made wine to be used in rituals. Both tribes, sharing similar ceremonies, worshipped two main divine beings – Elder Brother and Earthmaker.

Traditional horned toad on Pima basket

ENDLESS USES
As near unbreakable containers, baskets had endless uses. Bowl-shaped ones were used for storing maize, and wider, flatter ones for carrying fruit collected from the top of the saguaro cactus. Designs picturing animals began to emerge in the 1800s.

Feather-decorated hide covers this Papago wooden shield

THE ART OF BASKETMAKING
The skill of basketmaking became an art among the Pima. Traditional techniques involved close coils of willow, wound around bullrushes. Patterns were produced by adding pieces of the black devil's claw plant to make a striking contrast. Papago basketry also borrowed from Spanish designs. A basket was sometimes so large, the maker had to climb inside to finish it!

BRIDLE WEAR
The Papago were semi-nomadic with few water resources. Horses were useful for travelling between their summer field villages in the desert and their winter well villages near mountain springs.

Natural and dyed horsehair used to make this Papago bridle rein

MOCK BATTLES
Papago and Pima ceremonies included mock battles, where shields like this one were used. Though not fierce raiders like the Apache, they found war with other tribes was often unavoidable and were effective and successful warriors. In the American Civil War, the Pima defended Arizona on behalf of the Union, defeating Confederate forces. After 1865 they served as valued scouts for the US Army in its campaigns against the Apache.

SIMPLE BUT EXQUISITE
Like the other peoples of the Southwest, the Pima and Papago were potters. Compared with the Hopi and Zuni, however, their designs were much simpler.

Rounded bottom allowed this Papago pottery water jar to fit into a basketry ring on top of the head

Feathers
from a bird
of prey

Massed eagle
feathers decorate
top (and back) of
clown mask

Solid thread
construction
marks out
hole for eye

Papago clown
mask seen
from front

Rear view
of Papago
clown
mask

Flap, attached
to crown, hangs
down the back

SACRED CROP CEREMONY
Pima and Papago ceremonies
centred on the single most
important thing in their lives,
the successful raising of their
crops in an arid land. In each
village one man, named the
Keeper of the Smoke, was
in charge of the ceremonies.
Every fourth year both tribes
held a special celebration (called
the Viikita) for the harvest. Ritual
dancers – costumed and masked
as sacred clowns – acted out the
people's dependence on the land,
the weather, and the divine beings.

RAIN SPIRITS
Because they lived in the desert,
the Papago had ceremonies to bring
rain. They made special journeys to
where they believed the rain spirits
dwelt to beg them to return to the
tribal lands. Every summer the
Papago performed a ritual where
they drank huge quantities of cactus
wine, believing that an alcoholic
stupor drove out evil, which
pleased the rain spirits.

Black design on
front of canvas
hood (made
from a flour
bag) symbolizes
a rain cloud

Horsehair braid
decorated with
red cloth

Land of the totem poles

Raven above a bear

Abalone-inlaid, ivory handle

Map of North America showing the Northwest region

BETWEEN THE DARK FORESTS and the ocean's edge in the rainy Northwest there grew up an extraordinary culture almost untouched by Europeans until the late 1700s. The people of this area, divided into about 30 tribes, never developed agriculture, but were able to live comfortably from the teeming riches of the sea, the forest, and the rivers filled with salmon during their annual runs. The bountiful environment allowed time to develop a splendid art and a complex society of nobles, commoners, and slaves. Wealthy families, proud of their status, expressed it in sumptuous ceremonies and monumental artworks, especially the towering wooden totem poles.

Hide strap used to lash knife to wrist

Iron blade of Tlingit fighting knife

Elegantly carved fins on Haida halibut club

WAR PARTIES
Typical Northwest coast warfare was a quick raid for revenge or to acquire plunder and slaves. Among the northern tribes, war was also aimed at controlling more land by driving away the enemy. Warriors wore wooden helmets and body armour made from strips of wood joined with rawhide. Weapons were bows, clubs, and knives (above). War knives originally had blades of stone or bone, but later of traded iron, and were lashed to the wrist during battle.

HOOKED ON HALIBUT
The island-dwelling Haida relied on fishing. Halibut were caught by setting hooks close to the ocean bed. Once hauled to the surface, such fish had to be stunned immediately with clubs for, at up to 180 kg (400 lb), their struggles might upset the canoe. The canoe was literally dug out of a trunk of a giant cedar tree, the prow decorated with an elaborate abstract carving.

Carving represents a raven on the upper part of this Haida totem pole

Intricate carving adorns this model of a Haida tomb

PERIOD OF MOURNING
A dead Haida was mourned ceremonially in the home for a period of four to six days. The body was then placed in a grave box and taken out through a specially made exit. Finally, the remains were put in a grave house, perhaps as large as an ordinary home, and commemorated with a memorial post.

TOTEM POLE VILLAGE
Architecture was one of the great achievements of the Northwest coast peoples. The huge wooden houses, their walls of cedar planks fitted over a massive cedar framework, were designed by architects who supervised skilled artisans and gangs of labourers, often slaves from other tribes. Several related families lived in a house. Living space reflected rank, the highest place of honour being the back wall. Like a second forest, totem poles dotted the village – some were built into the house's front, the door a hole at the base. Free-standing poles were often memorials.

Small frog carving

A FAMILY'S STATUS
Totem poles were not idols, as Christian missionaries believed, but monuments proclaiming a family's status by recording its family tree. Every household claimed through its legends a relationship with a spirit being in the form of an animal, such as a raven, wolf, bear, or eagle. Carvings representing these beings were family crests, much like a coat of arms in medieval Europe.

Totem pole carved from a trunk of a cedar tree

Lower carvings on totem pole depict marriage alliances or other important family events

This pole is 6 m (20 ft) long, but a whole totem pole could stand over 12 m (40 ft) high

SMOKING PIPES
Tlingit men never smoked until they obtained tobacco from white traders, c. 1800. Then they began to produce an astonishing variety of intricately carved wooden pipes with metal bowls, used only by men as women did not smoke. Designs depicted crests – this Tlingit example has two carved wooden wolves, painted, and inlaid with abalone shells.

Horned owl carved on top third of totem pole

Head of bird of prey

Represents feathers of a bird

Small Haida totem pole or grave post

SECRETS BEHIND TOTEM POLES
Wealthy families commissioned sculptors to carve totem poles for various purposes, mostly related to mortuary rites and memorials to the dead. The heir of a deceased chief might erect a pole in his honour as part of the process of taking over his role and titles. Sometimes, the dead chief's remains were interred in a box on top of a pole. Raising a totem pole was always accompanied by the great ceremony of potlatch.

Art second to none

IN THE FLICKERING FIRELIGHT of a Northwest house during the winter ceremonies, two great arts were dramatically displayed together – ritual dances and intricately carved masks. The dances, held by secret societies to initiate a new member, re-enacted the links between ancestors and spirit beings. Masked dancers represented the power and continuing presence of the spirit world. The ceremony was both ritual and theatre, for the dancers used spectacular special effects to enhance the story they were telling. Membership of the societies, the right to dance, and possession of the masks helped define privileges in this status-conscious culture. Both male and female shamans, in their role as doctors, also wore ritual masks.

Open Kwakiutl transformation mask

Interior image represents spirit of clan ancestor

Cord, looping through eye and cheek bones, is pulled to open up the mask

Haida wooden rattle in form of a hawk

Bar supplies leverage to pull open the beak

When closed, this Kwakiutl transformation mask looks like an eagle's head

Abalone shell forming the bird's eye

SHAMANS' RATTLES
Shamans were revered by the tribe because of their awesome powers. These derived from special access to the spirit world through a personal guardian spirit, summoned by singing and the shaking of a sacred rattle. Illness was thought to be caused either by the intrusion of a small object into the body or by the loss or theft of the soul. Spirits, often manipulated by witches, were perhaps behind much illness. In a dramatic ceremony that involved a fee, a shaman cured by removing the object or by restoring the lost soul. The witch was then identified and punished.

SECRET SOCIETIES
The Kwakiutl, who probably began the secret societies which eventually spread across the Northwest, had three – the Shaman Society, representing violent and threatening spirits; the Dluwulaxa, linked to the sky spirits; and the Nutlam, whose ancestor was the wolf spirit. Most important to the Shaman Society was a cannibal spirit – the dancers in this ceremony, called Hamatsa, had great prestige and wore particularly elaborate masks. The object of the Kwakiutls' Winter Rituals, which continued for four months from mid-November, was to establish a connection between uninitiated youths and a particular supernatural being, after which the youths became members of the appropriate secret society.

Three witches planning evil activities, being guarded by an octopus near handle

Dead man with protruding tongue in bill of kingfisher

Red ball is the Sun, once stolen but now raven is releasing it to light up the world

Tlingit wooden raven rattle

Tlingit shaman's wooden oyster catcher rattle

Spirit represented in quasi-human form

Painting inside bird's head shows internal view of eye, nostril, and beak

BEHIND THE MASK

Separate from the winter ceremonies were those which displayed the household's privileges. This spectacular Kwakiutl transformation mask (changing from a bird's face into a human one) was probably part of such a dance. It was fixed to the dancer's head by a frame of wickerwork and animal sinews. The two bars at the back were linked by draw-cords to the sides of the beak, a third cord to the lower part of the beak. Manipulating the cords transformed in a moment an eagle spirit into one with a fierce human face.

Head has human features except for hooked beak rather than a nose

Bella Coola Sun Mask

Four oval faces, each flanked by a pair of upraised hands, surround the Sun

RED AS THE SUN

The Bella Coola lived in northern British Columbia, between two groups of the Kwakiutl. Membership of their Dance Society, usually hereditary, was a coveted privilege because it brought great status. At their four-night winter ceremony, members performed dances taught to them by the spirit beings of the sky. Wearing masks representing the spirits, the dancers acted out with great drama the central stories of the tribe's beliefs. Masks were carved to give a striking effect, so that identifying a certain spirit was sometimes difficult.

Carved, painted spherical face represents the Spirit of the Sun

The power of potlatch

IN THE NORTHWEST, gaining wealth brought the possibility of status but, in the great potlatch ceremonies, giving wealth away guaranteed it. Potlatches were lavish distributions of gifts from host to guests (who could number in the hundreds) and took place in order to gain acceptance for a change in status or acquisition of privileges. Potlatches did not bankrupt the giver because being host at one guaranteed being a guest and, therefore, a receiver of gifts at others. In a society of often intense rivalries, potlatches syphoned off the tensions which otherwise might have led to war. Potlatches still persist. A Canadian government ban, from 1884 to 1951, was defied by the Kwakiutl and there has been a general revival of the ceremony since the 1960s.

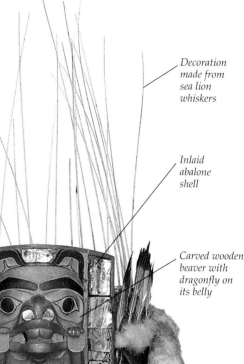

Decoration made from sea lion whiskers

Inlaid abalone shell

Carved wooden beaver with dragonfly on its belly

Woodpecker feather

Luxurious Haida headdress displays wealth of its owner

Ermine pelt

HAIDA HEADDRESS
Much of the artistic activity among Northwest coast tribes went into creating their magnificent potlatch costumes. In the 1800s, the Haida copied headdresses for ceremonial dances from more northern tribes. Such a headdress (above) would have been worn in association with a Chilkat blanket (below).

Image of family crest engraved on this 1-m (3-ft) high Haida copper

MOST PRECIOUS POSSESSION
Engraved metal, shield-shaped plaques called coppers were thought immensely valuable and highly prized as a potlatch gift. Although coppers, as symbols of wealth, were invented by the Northwest coast tribes before the arrival of the Europeans, they became even more popular later during the 19th-century fur trade period because of the tribes' easy access to copper.

Chief Tutlidi and son at Fort Rupert in 1894

BESTOWING A COPPER
The gift of a copper demonstrated great wealth and thus earned prestige, honouring both giver and receiver. Alternatively, in a flamboyant gesture, a chief might deliberately break a copper, as shown on the left where a chief is giving away a copper in honour of his son and heir. Rivalry between chiefs was often intense, so one might break a copper and give the pieces to his rival. The recipient was at once expected to break one of equal or greater value, or be shamed.

DRESSED FOR A POTLATCH

Chilkat blankets and dancing dresses (right) were highly valued. They were woven from mountain goat's wool and cedar bark by Tlingit women. The weavers were paid a high fee, so possession of such objects showed the owner's wealth. The dresses were passed on to relatives and were ostentatiously displayed at potlatches, where a host honoured his guests by giving them pieces cut from his dress.

Every ring denotes that the wearer had hosted one potlatch

Symbolic crest design, provided by the men, who painted it onto a board for the women weavers

A CEREMONIAL HAT

Potlatches were held to celebrate the marriage of a chief, to inaugurate a new clan house, or to mark the death of an old chief. The chief of a household was responsible for managing its harvest from sea and forest (from which he took a share) and for relations with other households. At potlatches, a host wearing ceremonial hat (left) and costume had help from a speaker, who made the formal announcements, and a master of ceremonies, who invited the many guests.

Ermine pelt decoration

WHAT A FEAST!

Potlatches were accompanied by a spectacular feast which might last for up to 12 days. The host tried to provide more food than could be eaten by his guests, who paid respect by eating until they were sick. Food included seal meat, fish, berries, and vegetables served with fish oil in vessels like this large, bear-shaped example.

Tlingit bear-shaped wooden bowl with shell inlays

Stylized bear carved into Tlingit feast dish

A WORK OF ART

Feast dishes were elaborately carved works of art, part of the visible symbols of a household's rank and wealth. The largest, which could be the size (and the shape) of a small canoe, were placed in front of the guest chiefs, who ate from them using spoons of mountain goat horn or wood. Ordinary guests had their food ladled into smaller dishes, like this Tlingit example (above).

Thin strands of spruce roots used in making this Tlingit basketry hat

Painting of crow depicts a family crest

This hat usually made in rainy weather to prevent materials drying out

Northern hunters

Map of North America showing the Subarctic region

LIFE IN THE SUBARCTIC demanded extraordinary ingenuity, courage, and self-reliance. Summers were short, winters ferocious, in the far northern forests and on the tundra. In this hard land, the search for food dominated life. All 30 Subarctic tribes survived by hunting and fishing, adapting to a nomadic life. The Chipewyan depended on caribou and followed the great herds on their seasonal migrations. Thc Ojibwa were forest hunters, moving between summer and winter camps. The Naskapi of the taiga (coniferous forests) relied on caribou and all kinds of game, like moose and beaver. Meat and fish were preserved by sun-drying or smoking. Hallmarks of the region were wigwams, snowshoes, the birchbark canoe, and skin clothing.

Hood on Ojibwa child's winter coat protects face from severe cold and wind

Hide fastening

A CHARMED HEAD
Though hunted, bears were regarded with awe by the Subarctic peoples who believed they possessed powerful spirits. Skulls were thought to retain the bear's spirit so they were kept as charms. A hunter would always pray to apologize to a bear's spirit, explaining his need for food, and for future successful hunts.

Simple decoration on Cree skull denoted a special honour to the bear's spirit

Strips of rabbitskin woven together

WARM WINTER WRAP
Winter clothing, generally made of tanned caribou skins with hair side inward, consisted of coats, mittens, leggings or trousers, moccasins, and hoods. Children sometimes wore winter coats woven from strips of rabbitskin. There were big differences between eastern and western tribes in styles of decoration. For example, easterners painted unique red designs on their coats, while those in the far west used porcupine quills, shells, and beads.

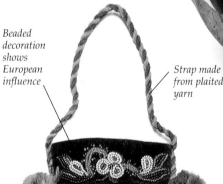

Beaded decoration shows European influence

Strap made from plaited yarn

Sharp end of caribou bone for scraping away flesh

Slavey tobacco pouch

A BEAR-FUR BAG
Spirits (both benevolent and malign) were placated through prayers and offerings of tobacco – the smoke rising to comfort the spirits. Tobacco was important in religious and ceremonial life. It was often presented as an invitation to a ceremony or feast and a gift of tobacco was accepted by the recipient as a great honour.

SKIN DRESSING
Preparing caribou skins was a woman's job, and a long and messy one. Split caribou bones, like this Chipewyan set, were used to scrape away any flesh – and outer hair, if not needed. A soup of rotting caribou brains was next rubbed into the skin for a smelly but effective tanning process. After washing, the skin was stretched on a frame and dried, then pulled and worked by hand until pliable. Last, it was smoked over a fire for a final curing.

Naskapi adult's snowshoe

Netting lashed to frame

MOOSE HUNTING
In this detail of a George Catlin painting, the hunter is on snowshoes and holding a spear in his hand. He is gliding easily through the snow drifts in pursuit of moose. A windy day deadened the sound of the snowshoes, while sunny weather helped harden the animals' footprints in the snow, making it easier to track them.

Netting separated by using wooden or bone needles

Rawhide netting often made of moose skin

Hide thongs for tying snowshoe to foot

MAKING A SNOWSHOE
Snowshoe frames were made from a long piece of birch, bent by steam to soften and shape it, then dried and seasoned. Next crossbars were slotted into the frame. The netting (called babiche) was cut in continuous strips from rawhide. Shapes developed to meet different sorts of country and types of snow. In the far north, shoes were long and narrow, but in the east and south they were oval or round – as shown in this Cree child's snowshoe.

Birch frame

IN DEEP SNOW
Snowshoes allowed the Subarctic peoples to extend their hunting and seasonal migrations into areas otherwise made impassable by deep snow. Moose hunting in winter depended on snowshoes. The hunter could follow the animals easily by their tracks and glide swiftly across the surface of drifts which bogged the moose down.

TRANSPORT BY TOBOGGAN
For transporting goods over snow, toboggans eased the strain on a human's back. Subarctic toboggans were usually made of split-log boards, steam-curled at the front to ride over the snow, and varying in length up to as much as 2.5 m (8 ft). Toboggans were usually hauled by men though some tribes, like the Ojibwa, used dogs. However, the Naskapi despised their hereditary foes, the Inuit, for using dog sleds.

SUMMER ENCAMPMENT ON CANADA'S LAKE HURON
Canadian artist Paul Kane (1810–71) painted this impression of an Ojibwa summer camp (detail above) in the mid-1800s. The Ojibwa left their winter camps in late March to spend the summer fishing, berry picking, harvesting wild rice, and living in birchbark wigwams.

Model of Naskapi man from eastern Canada hauling a toboggan

The frozen Arctic

OUTSIDERS THOUGHT the Arctic (from Greenland to Siberia) was a terrifying trackless ice-desert, but the Inuit made it their home. They lived from the treeless tundra, with winter temperatures of -46°C (-50°F), to the shores of the Arctic Ocean, which froze to a depth of 2 m (6 ft). The Inuit thus proved that human beings are the most adaptable of Earth's creatures. They built a way of life on hunting seal, walrus, whale, and caribou and developed the world's most efficient cold-weather clothing and housing (like the famous igloo made of blocks of snow piled in a narrowing spiral). On land, they used fast dog sleds and at sea skin boats – either single kayaks or the umiak, used for hunting the largest sea mammals.

Map of North America showing the Arctic region

Bowstring made from twisted sinew

Strips of hide to improve the hand grip

Copper Inuit bow and arrow

Bone foreshaft lashed to shaft with thin strips of sinew

Copper tip

Feather flight

Ivory handle

Steel blade

THE HUNTING SEASONS

Inuit winter camps were on the sea ice where they hunted sea mammals, especially seal. In summer they moved inland to fish and hunt. September was the climax of the summer hunt when great herds of caribou assembled to migrate south. The Inuit left their summer camps to follow the herds, killing large numbers for food and hides for winter clothing. Favourite hunting techniques were to spear or shoot caribou from kayaks as they swam in small lakes, or to stampede them into ambushes where they could be shot with arrows at close range.

ALL-PURPOSE KNIFE

Skinning and butchering seals was a woman's task. She used an ulu – a semi-circular knife with a wooden or horn handle. An all-purpose tool, it was also used for scraping skins and in cooking.

Baffin Inuit harpoon

Bowdrill used to carve ivory cribbage board, c. 1902

Bone mouth piece

Rawhide bowstring wrapped around shaft

Bow

Coiled hide line

Wooden shaft rotated by moving the bow

Southampton Inuit bow and arrow

WINTER WALRUS HUNTING

The Inuit hunted walrus for dog meat, hides for covering umiaks, and ivory from the tusks for decorative carving. One way was to harpoon them from umiaks, then lancing the exhausted animals to death. The other was to hunt walrus basking on the ice or lure walrus swimming close to the ice's edge. Then the walrus was harpooned, the butt of the harpoon anchored in the ice, and the harpoon line fastened at the butt. The harpoon became a powerful lever – even a walrus could not escape. The walrus gradually tired and was drawn close to the waiting hunter so it could be lanced.

MAKING FIRE

The Inuit produced fire with the bowdrill. It could be used either as a simple drilling tool or for firemaking. Spinning the shaft against the base piece made sawdust, which was then ignited by the heat generated by the continuing friction.

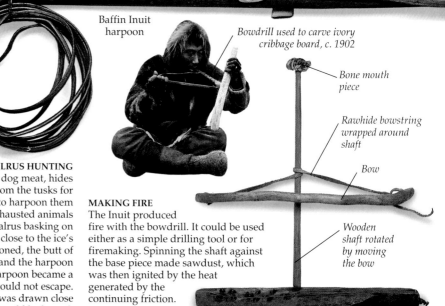

Hood could be pulled up for maximum protection in rough seas

Waterproof anorak made from strips of seal intestine tightly sewn together

Decoration of feathers and orange beaks from tiny birds

PERFECT INSULATION
Inuit clothing is light but provides excellent insulation. The hooded anorak is made from animal skins, itself air-tight but trapping a layer of insulating air against the body. Loose at the bottom, it can be ventilated periodically if the wearer starts to perspire by pulling the anorak forward at the neck – hot air escapes upward and cold air enters at the bottom. Kayak hunters tied their anoraks round the rim of the manhole to keep out the wet. Some also wore waterproof anoraks made from seal intestines (right).

Bottom of anorak tied to rim of kayak for extra waterproofing

Southampton, Baffin, and West Alaska Inuit snow goggles (top to bottom)

ARCTIC SUNGLASSES
Arctic peoples invented sunglasses long before Europeans. Snow and ice glare could cause temporary blindness. Wood or bone goggles, blackened on the inside, blocked most sunlight. Vision was through a narrow horizontal slit.

Hide strip lashes wooden shaft to ivory foreshaft

Metal harpoon point and ivory head become detached from foreshaft after thrust – as animal struggles, head pivots side-ways in wound

West Alaska Inuit finger mask decorated with fur and feathers

Feathers decorate West Alaska Inuit painted wooden helmet

Carved ivory decoration

KEEPING THE SUN OFF
In the summer seal hunts, the Inuit used kayaks – fast, lightweight canoes, easily manoeuvred by one person. With little or no access to timber, they used driftwood for the frame, then covered it with dressed seal skin, which was waterproofed with seal oil. To protect their eyes from the sun's glare off the water and drifting ice floes, hunters wore wooden helmets, often beautifully decorated.

CEREMONIAL MASKS
At Inuit rituals male dancers wore wooden face masks representing the spirits of creatures or natural forces, as seen in visions by the shamans. The women wore finger masks (tiny replicas of the men's masks), which focused attention on their flowing hand gestures.

Modern times

THE "VANISHING INDIAN" was how Native North Americans were regarded a century ago. They were expected eventually to join white North American society, or simply die out – but they have refused to do either. Now numbering 2.5 million in the USA and Canada, over half living outside reservations, Native North Americans are reviving tribal traditions and seeking their own role in a multi-cultural nation. Canadian and US government policy, even when well-intentioned, tended to make reservations dependent on government support, while tribal resources were plundered by business interests. Despair brought unemployment, disease, and lack of education far higher than the national average. From the 1970s, militant protests dramatized key issues, but have been less effective than using the law to force compensation for lost rights. Today, many Native North Americans hope to bring back traditional forms of decision-making and leadership.

Modern interpretation of traditional Mohawk hairstyle

Coca-Cola bottle on a pedestal

Mohawk spirit motif

WALKING HIGH STEEL
Mohawks from the Northeast are famous for their dangerous and highly skilled work in erecting bridges and skyscrapers. An original twelve, hired in 1886, taught relatives and friends how to "walk the high steel". The 1930s' New York skyscraper boom created a Mohawk community which continues to sell its remarkable skills today. Old traditions of bravery and kinship thus operate in a modern industry.

MODERN ART
Native North American identity can today inspire an artist but need not dictate his subjects. Former high-steel worker, Richard Glazer Danay, painted this "hard hat" as a modern Mohawk headdress. He mixes sarcastic images of American life, classical art allusions, and motifs echoing Mohawk traditions.

Modern Mohawk "headdress" painted by Native American artist, Richard Glazer Danay in 1982

Figure alludes to a Renaissance painting

ANCIENT CEREMONIES

Traditional ceremonies retain force and meaning for the Apache. Dancers (left), wearing symbolic masks, headdresses, and body paint, represent Gans (mountain spirit beings). Directed by a shaman, the Gans' impersonators perform rituals to gain protection against hostile spirits or to heal the sick. Also Gans dancers may provide entertainment at the four-day celebrations marking a girl's coming of age.

Navajo woman baking bread, using traditional oven and equipment

CARRYING ON TRADITIONS

Over 200,000 Navajo live on their 6-million-ha (15-million-acre) reservation chiefly in Arizona – the largest in the USA. The Navajo have long been divided over how far to accept white American ways. The tribal council still holds meetings in Navajo, and ceremonies (particularly those for curing illness) remain central to tribal life. Traditional Navajo art, such as weaving and silverwork, is an important source of income.

SOCIAL BENEFITS

Using their rights over their own lands, confirmed by a 1988 Act of Congress, Native Americans have opened gambling casinos in 33 states across the USA. Casinos provide jobs and profits pay for housing, schools, and health care. However, arguments over how to spend the money have already divided tribes and some leaders fear gambling will have bad social effects.

THE POWER OF POWWOW

Though never abandoned, powwows have again become hugely popular. Nearly 1,000 in 1993, attended by 90 per cent of Native North Americans, they are a way of asserting Native peoples' identity. Many tribes participate in these weekend celebrations with the focus on dancing. Social dances ("Intertribals") are mixed with traditional competition dances.

Group of Ojibwa children at a powwow

GETTING AN EDUCATION

From the 1960s Canadian and US governments have provided funds for new education programmes run by the tribes themselves. New schools (teaching in both the tribal language and English) mean that nearly all reservation children now attend school.

NORTHWEST TERRITORIES TRIBAL MEETING

In the 1970s new legal help groups, such as the Native American Rights Fund, won cases before the (US) Indian Claims Commission, first set up in 1946. It now settled land claims arising from broken treaties – the Lakota received $105 million and tribes in Maine were awarded $40 million. The Canadian government and the Inuit agreed a new self-governing Inuit territory (Nunavut) in 1991.

Index

Catalogue numbers of artefacts photographed at the AMNH:

1. 50.1/2448. 2. tl 50.1/1331; tc E/2565; tr 50/3084; cl 50.1/1205; c 50.1/316; CR 60–53; cb 50/3808; bc 50/9789AB. 3. tl 50/7649; tr 16/902; b 50/5545, 5546. 4. tl 50/355; tc 50/7388; tr 50/3045; cl 1/2082; clb 50.1/954; bl 50/8405; bc 50/8196; br 50/9485, H/15179. 5. tr 50/5719. 6. cl 20.2/2778; tr 20.2/5865, 20.1/8577; c DN/756; br T/2448, 20/6871, T/914, 20/6795. 7. tl H/5144; tc 29.1/6070; cl H/10426; cr 29.1/7105; bl 29.1/341. 8. l 50.2/1182A; br 50/9173. 9. t E/419; br 50/7649. 10. l 16/4921; cl 50.1/5418; br 16/535, 16.1/769, 16/534. 11. tl 50/5449A; br 50.1/5466A–H. 12. tr 50.1/7475; cl 50.1/6443; b 1/4133. 13. tl 50.2/1320; cr 50/7388; cbr 50.1/7607AB. 14. l 50.1/1696; ctl 50.1/1768. 15. tl 50.1/1744; r 50.1/1528. 16. ctr 50.1/5651, 50.1/1544; c 50/3706, 50/6870; bl 50.1/5632A, 50/6188H; br 50.1/5648, 50.1/1852. 17. tl 50/6486; cr 50.1/1908; bl 50.1/1786, NAE/0064, 50.1/1886. 18. tr 50.1/1942; cbl 50.1/1943, 50.1/1595; bl 50.1/1603; br 50.1/7572. 19. tl 50.1/1613AB, 50.1/1614AB. 20. tr 50.1/6609; cl NN1–4; b T/833. 21. tl 50.1/8657; tc 50.1/7038; tr 10/34. 22. tr 50.1/2232; cl 50.1/7174AB; bl 50/9950, 50/9949, 50/572; br 50.2/1378. 23. tr 50.1/6625; br 50/4695AB. 24. cr 50/5336; b 50.1/7215. 25. tl 20.0/713; tc D/N116; tr 50/5816; ct 50/5363; cb 50/5364. 26. l 50/3808; tr 50.2/6405, 50.2/6407; c 50/7306. 27. l 50/5323. 28. 50.1/516, 50.1/507, 508. 29. tl 50.1/5768AB; cl 50.2/2878; tr 50/301, 50/301A–C. 30. cl 50.1/7515. 31. tl 50/5740; bl 50/5756; r 50.1/392, 50.2/6554, 50.1/301, 50.1/323AB, 50.1/8035AB. 32. l 50.1/5432. 33. cr 50.1/6012; r 50.1/7894. 34. cl 1/4606; tr 50/5545. 35. tl 50/5760; br 50/5546. 36. tr 50/5719; bl 50.1/5652AB; br 50.1/4011A. 37. tr 50/6166D. 38. t 16/8648; c 16/8649, 8650A–F; cr 16/9076, 16/9077A; bl 50/3768. 39. l 16/1285; c 16/8666; br 50/2515. 40. cb 50/9268; bl 50.2/6786. 41. l 50.1/5991; cr 50/1275AB; bl 50.2/3470AB. 42. cl 50/3132; bl 1/4681, 4682; r 50/2612. 43. tl 50/565; tr 50/2588; cr T/18243; br 50/3178, 50/3431, 50.1/2038B. 44. l 50.1/9232; c 50.2/4760; cr 50.1/4049; b 50.1/9218. 45. t 50.1/2448. 46. l 50/9485, H/15179; cl H/15199; tr 50.2/5664; r 50/9523. 47. tr 50.2/6593; l 50/9433; r 50/9318. 48. tl 50.2/4817; bl 50/8629; c 50.1/6213AB; cr 50/8405; r 50.1/954. 49. l 50.2/4819A–D; br 50.2/4819E; br 50/8196. 50. tr 50.1/4191; bl 50.1/4776; br 50.1/4889; r 50.1/4182. 51. c, bl 50.1/4592. 52. tl E/1525; cl 16/16B; b 16/949. 53. tr E/806; l 16.1/558B; r 16/8686. 54. tr, cl 16/6770; cr 16/308; bc E/348; br 19/803. 55. br 16/7507. 56. tr 16/245; bl 16.1/404. 57. l 19/1000; tr 19/1048; c 19/1086; br 19/1239. 58. tr 50.2/3008; c 50/7028; bl 50/7722; br 50/7108, 7109. 59. tl 50.2/2736B; cr 50/7018B. 60. l 60/2477, 60/2478A; cl 60.2/5371, 60/6975D; cr 60.1/5361; cb 60/1133–4; br 60/3ABC. 61. t 60.2/5500; cr 60/5269, 60/3336B, 60/1355; cbr 60.1/3996; b 60.1/3773.

Acknowledgements

Dorling Kindersley would like to thank: The American Museum of Natural History, especially Anibal Rodriguez and Judith Levinson (Anthropology); John Davey (Publications); Deborah Barral, Mark Gostnell, Lize Mogel, Alan Walker, Marco Hernandez, and Rob Muller (Exhibitions); Joe Donato, Tony Macaluso, Martin Daly, Eadwinn Brookes, and Aldwin Phillip (Electricians); Eddy Garcia (Maintenance). Leslie Gerhauser, photographic assistance. Sally Rose, additional research. Helena Spiteri, Tim Button, Sophy D'Angelo, Ivan Finnegan, Kati Poynor, and Susan St. Louis for editorial and design assistance. Dave King and Kate Warren for extra photography, Museum of Mankind. **Artwork:** John Woodcock

Picture credits
(t=top b=bottom c=centre l=left r=right a=above)
American Indian Contemporary Art: Larry McNeil, 62bl. American Museum of Natural History: 36tl (no. 335493), 43cb (no. 2A342), 52cbr (no. 44309), 56cbr (no. 121545); E.S. Curtis 39tr (no. 335534), 46tl (no. 335553A); J.K. Dixon 28b (no. 316642). Bridgeman Art Library: D.F. Barry, Bismarck, Dakota 31c; British Museum 18c; Private Collection 32c; Royal Ontario Museum, Toronto 59cbr. Trustees of The British Museum: 9cl, 9c. Colorific!/Black Star: J. Cammick 63cl; P.S. Mecca 62r. Comstock: Georg Gerster 45cb. Hutchison Libary: Moser 63br. The Image Bank: Marvin Newman 63tl. Ann Ronan Image Select: 16tr. Collections of the Library of Congress: 30cr. Magnum Photos: E. Arnold 63tr. Mansell Collection: 25cbr, 25b, 49cr. Minnesota Historical Society: 33c. Montana Historical Society, Helena: 34tr. Nevada Historical Society, Reno: 40cra, 41tr. Peter Newark's Western Americana: jacket, 10ca, 10cb, 12ca, 14tl, 19tr, 21br, 23tl, 27cr, 28c, 33tl, 34c, 37bl, 40tl, 46clb. The Arizona Historical Society, Tucson 48tr. Rochester Museum and Science Center, Rochester, NY: (Formation of the League, Ernest Smith) 14cr. Royal Ontario Museum, Toronto: (detail from Hunting Moose Deer in Winter) 59tr. Service de la Marine, Vincennes: (detail from Culture & Stationis Ratio, de Bry) 17br. Smithsonian Institution: Department of Anthropology 30/31 (cat. no. 358425); National Anthropological Archives 19br, 26bc, 27tcr, 30tr, 35tr, 41tl, 42cra, 50cra, 60bcr. Courtesy of The Southwest Museum, Los Angeles: 22c. Frank Spooner Pictures/Gamma: A. Ribeiro 63cr. Trip/Eye Ubiquitous: L Fordyce 63bc. Every effort has been made to trace the copyright holders of photographs. The publishers apologize for any omissions and will amend further editions.